Zaner-Bloser
Handwriting

D1307323

Zaner-Bloser
The Language Arts and Reading Company

Senior Consultant

Steve Graham, Ed.D., Currey Ingram Professor of Special Education and Literacy, Vanderbilt University

Occupational Therapy Consultants

Jane Case-Smith, Ed.D., OTR/L, FAOTA, Chair of the Occupational Therapy Division, Ohio State University

Mary Benbow, M.S., OTR, La Jolla, CA

Asha Asher, MA OTR/L, FAOTA, M.Ed. (Special Education), Cincinnati, OH

North Shore Pediatric Therapy

ELL Consultants

Ellen Riojas Clark, Ph.D., Professor of Bicultural-Bilingual Studies, University of Texas at San Antonio

Bertha Pérez, Ed.D., Professor Emeritus of Literacy, University of Texas at San Antonio

Consultant

Debbie Diller, Educational Consultant, Houston, TX

Occupational Therapy Advisory Board

Kathleen A. Benton-Sanchez, M.P.A., OTR/L, Nashville, TN

Sherry Eisenbach, OT/L, Portland, OR

Elizabeth Gerich, OTR/L, Plymouth, MN

Sheila Martins, OTR/L, North Las Vegas, NV

Carol Miller, OTR/L, Marietta, OH

Leslie N. Parker, OTR/L, Huntington, WV

Tricia Shibuya, OTR/L, Las Vegas, NV

Denaysa Sisemore, M.S., OTR/L, Windsor, CO

Cheryl Weaver, CAS, M.S.Ed., OTR/L, Macedon, NY

Reviewers

Amy Bass, National Heritage Academies, Byron Center, MI

Donetta S. Brown, Birmingham City Schools, AL

Kelly Caravelli, Poway Unified School District, San Diego, CA

Michelle Corsi, East Windsor Regional Schools, NJ

Naomi Drewitz, East Windsor Regional Schools, NJ

Shan Glandon, Tulsa, OK

Karen Jackson, School District of Philadelphia, PA

Liz Knowles, Ed.D., 21st Century Curriculum Designs, LLC, Del Ray Beach, FL

Rita Olsen, Chicago Public Schools, IL

Geraldine A. Pappas, Detroit Public Schools, MI

Michael E. Pizzingrillo, Roman Catholic Diocese of Brooklyn, NY

Deborah C. Thomas, Ed.D., Montgomery Public Schools, AL

Ellen Lerch Thomsen, Roanoke County Public Schools, VA

Iefay Williams, School District of Philadelphia, PA

Credits

Photo: ©Corbis/SuperStock: Z3; ©Jon Parker Lee/Alamy: Z7; ©George Anderson Photography: Z21

ISBN 978-0-7367-6852-8

Zaner-Bloser, Inc.
800.421.3018
www.zaner-bloser.com

Printed in the United States of America   11 12 13 14 15 330 7 6 5 4 3

Certified Chain of Custody
SUSTAINABLE FORESTRY INITIATIVE
Promoting Sustainable Forest Management
www.sfiprogram.org

Zaner-Bloser
Handwriting
Shaping Effective Communicators

Z2

Table of Contents

Everything you need to confidently teach handwriting!

Zaner-Bloser Handwriting is a complete program that
- can be taught in 15 minutes a day.
- provides easy-to-use digital resources to engage students and support teachers.
- uses academic language and modeling with fewer, more specific stroke descriptions than other programs.
- teaches vertical manuscript, rather than a modified italic letterform, to better promote early literacy development.
- embeds professional development to fully support English Language Learners at all stages of language acquisition.

Parallel Spanish instruction is available for Grades K–3. See page Z19.

Zaner-Bloser Handwriting provides a full selection of classroom, multisensory, and optional practice materials. See page Z17.

Zaner-Bloser Handwriting encourages students and teachers to develop, celebrate, and reward legible handwriting through the annual Zaner-Bloser National Handwriting Contest. See page Z24.

Zaner-Bloser Handwriting has been the leading handwriting curriculum supporting students and teachers for over 120 years.

Z3

Communication

Strong communication skills make a world of difference. And with explicit handwriting instruction, your students can become more effective communicators.

It's proven that better handwriting skills lead to better literacy skills...

Developmentally appropriate handwriting instruction delivered in a consistent, ongoing manner, is a proven critical component of overall literacy development.

With **Zaner-Bloser Handwriting ©2012** you will

- **support early reading and writing development through print awareness and improved letter recognition.**
Zaner-Bloser's vertical manuscript alphabet improves letter recognition and supports reading development because it is the same letterform students see inside and outside the classroom every day. Vertical manuscript is the most widely used letterform in environmental print.

- **strengthen students' ability to self-regulate.**
As students practice, evaluate, and improve their handwriting, they realize the value of self-evaluation in all of their written work.

- **encourage ongoing literacy growth to improve written communications.**
As students master the fundamentals of handwriting, they are able to form letters quickly, fluently, and legibly—leaving them free to focus on the process and content of their writing.

- **reduce the need for handwriting-related intervention.**
Promote better handwriting for all students and reduce the need for costly occupational therapy referrals. Built-in multisensory activities, coaching, and corrective strategies are included in every Teacher Edition.

...and better literacy skills lead to more effective communication.

With **Zaner-Bloser Handwriting,** you will provide your students with a vital literacy skill. What's more, you'll develop your students' ability and confidence to write in any situation—from the highly personal to the very public. So whether your students are writing a simple thank-you note, taking notes in class, or composing an essay on the computer, together we'll be shaping effective communicators for today's world.

Program Components

Student Edition
- Includes easy, step-by-step instruction and self-evaluation.
- Provides meaningful practice and application.
- Engages students with colorful, fun activities.

Teacher Edition
- Includes full annotation.
- Offers easy, step-by-step guide with embedded professional development.

Practice Masters
- Provides more practice for every letter and skill.
- Offers school-to-home activities and letters.
- Available on CD-ROM.

a vital skill in today's world

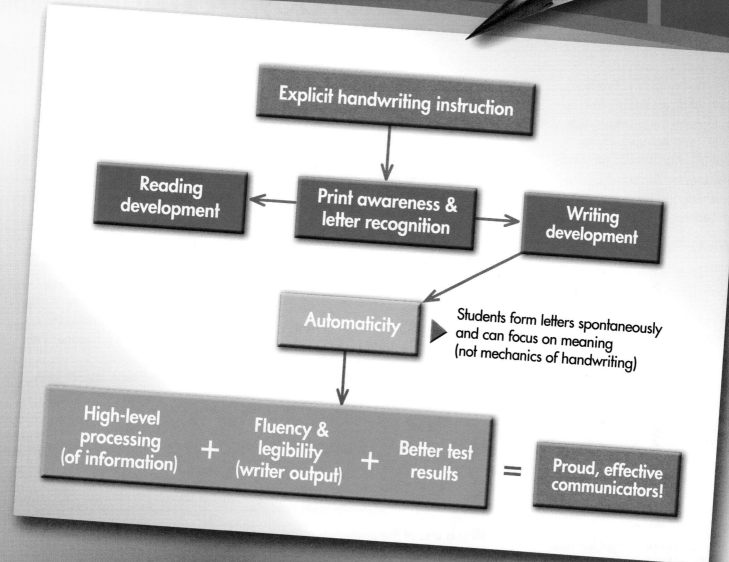

Explicit handwriting instruction

→

Print awareness & letter recognition

← Reading development

→ Writing development

Automaticity

▶ Students form letters spontaneously and can focus on meaning (not mechanics of handwriting)

High-level processing (of information)

+

Fluency & legibility (writer output)

+

Better test results

=

Proud, effective communicators!

Poster Super Pack

The perfect addition to the handwriting classroom. Includes:

- Manuscript and Cursive alphabet posters
- Keys to Legibility poster
- Handwriting Positions poster

Digital Resources for Handwriting

Multimedia lessons and interactive letter practice make handwriting easy and fun. See pages Z16–Z17 for a complete list of optional support materials.

La escritura

- Offers parallel handwriting instruction in Spanish.
- Student Edition, Teacher Guide, and Practice Masters available for Grades K–3.

Handwriting: A Basic Building Block of Literacy

By Steve Graham, Ed.D.

We all love to play with letters, making and remaking words with them through anagrams, crossword puzzles, and games such as Scrabble®. Kids love to play with letters, too, as illustrated by the three childhood jokes below (from Lederer, 1998).

What letters hold nothing? **(MT)**

What letters name a slippery spot? **(IC)**

What begins with **t,** ends with **t,** and is full of **t**? (a **teapot** of course)

While letters can be fun, they are also serious business. The space probe *Mariner I,* bound for Venus, never reached its destination because of a single character missing from its programming code.

Letters bedevil more than just computer programmers. At some point, one or more letters probably got the best of you. They have certainly taken me down a time or two. Just recently, one of my students asked about a comment I had made on her paper. After studying it, I finally deciphered my cryptic note: "I can't read your writing—please write more legibly."

I am glad to say that I was able to see the humor in this situation, even though I was a little embarrassed by it. With any luck, my "stumble with letters" will be forgotten, leaving no visible imprint or consequences.

With children, letters cannot be treated lightly or forgotten— they are very serious business. How legibly and quickly students write letters influences their success in school.

One way that handwriting exerts its influence is through students' grades.

a less legible copy of it. This has been demonstrated repeatedly in scientific experiments.

Handwriting also plays a role in how students approach timed-writing assignments and tests. Students must decide whether to slow down and write more neatly or speed up to make sure they finish writing their response. If they go faster, legibility is likely to suffer, resulting in a lower grade. If they slow down and write more neatly, they run the risk of not finishing their response. This decision influences their grade as well.

> How legibly and quickly students write letters influences their success in school.

Writing is one of the primary ways teachers evaluate students' learning. You ask students to write answers to homework assignments, take written tests, and prepare reports to demonstrate what they know. A lower grade is inevitable if part or all of a writing assignment or test response is unreadable. Even when students produce legible writing, handwriting still influences the grade assigned. Higher grades are assigned to a more legible version of the same paper than

Handwriting further impacts students' grades through its effect on learning. Students with less legible or slower handwriting do not fully enjoy the positive benefits of using writing as a tool for learning. For example, studying for a test is more challenging if lecture and text notes are illegible or notes are incomplete due to slow handwriting.

The influence of handwriting extends beyond students' grades. It constrains and shapes children's writing.

Zaner-Bloser

Handwriting

Shaping Effective Communicators

Z6

For young writers, the physical act of transcribing words into text is so demanding, many children may minimize their use of other writing processes. They turn writing into a "knowledge telling" process in which an idea is generated and written on paper and each new idea serves as the stimulus for the next one. Mostly absent from this approach are other demanding mental processes, such as thinking about the needs of the reader or the organization of text. This makes it especially important that young writers learn to produce letters quickly and correctly with little effort, so they can devote more attention and mental resources to other aspects of writing.

The impact of handwriting is even more severe for students who struggle with mastering it. These children typically avoid writing whenever they can, developing the mindset that they cannot write, which increases the likelihood they will become poor writers.

I am sure you have encountered the sentiment: "Thanks to word processing, I don't need to teach handwriting." Unfortunately, this is simply not true. Most writing in school takes place by hand.

In 80 percent of elementary schools, students rarely if ever use word processing for writing (Cutler & Graham, 2008). Very few classes have enough computers to make regular use of word processors possible. In fact, handwriting is not about to disappear, as it is unlikely that anything will ever be as inexpensive as pen and paper.

Because handwriting is so important to school success, it cannot be taken for granted. Students must learn to write letters legibly and fluently. The best way to make sure this happens is to explicitly—and systematically—teach handwriting. There is a century's worth of research supporting the effectiveness of this tactic. Even for children with the poorest handwriting, I found that directly teaching this skill not only improves handwriting, but enhances how well these children write (Graham, Harris, & Fink, 2000).

I would like to end by coming full circle, leaving you with this letter puzzler:

> What occurs once in every minute, twice in every moment, but never in a thousand years?
>
> (Hint: The answer involves only a single letter.)

> Most writing in school takes place by hand. In 80 percent of elementary schools, students rarely if ever use word processing for writing.

References:

Cutler, L., & Graham, S. (2008). Primary grade writing instruction: A national survey. *Journal of Educational Psychology, 100*, 907–919.

Graham, S., Harris, K.R., & Fink, B. (2000). Is handwriting causally related to learning to write? Treatment of handwriting problems in beginning writers. *Journal of Educational Psychology, 92*, 620–633.

Lederer, R. (1998). *The word circus*. Springfield, MA: Merriam-Webster.

Steve Graham, Ed.D., is the Currey Ingram Professor of Special Education and Literacy at Vanderbilt University. His research interests include learning disabilities, writing instruction and writing development, and the development of self-regulation. Dr. Graham is the editor of *Exceptional Children* and coauthor of the *Handbook of Writing Research, Handbook of Learning Disabilities, Writing Better,* and *Making the Writing Process Work*. He received his Ed.D. in special education from the University of Kansas.

Answer: M

Student Edition

Students focus on letters with a common beginning stroke, such as undercurve, to reinforce correct letter formation.

Explicit, ongoing handwriting instruction is a critical component of students' overall literacy development. It provides a foundation for success in reading, writing, and test taking.

Zaner-Bloser Handwriting guides students through a proven, step-by-step process for learning legible handwriting, a vital literacy skill. The engaging, colorful Student Edition provides developmentally appropriate activities to

- increase legibility through regular self-evaluation.

- develop fluency and automaticity.

Letter models with arrows clearly show stroke sequence.

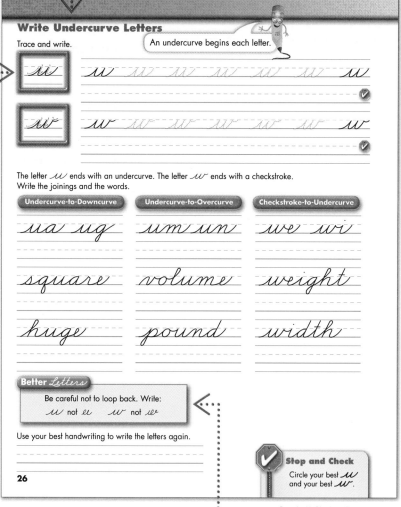

Grade 4 Student Edition page

Better Letters shows students common problems to avoid when writing letters and joinings.

Shaping Effective Communicators

Students practice writing letters, joinings, words, and sentences directly beneath a model that **both left- and right-handed** students can easily see.

High-frequency words are included to enhance reading development.

Trace and write.

An undercurve begins each letter.

The letters *e* and *l* end with an undercurve. Write the joinings and words.

Undercurve-to-Undercurve	Undercurve-to-Downcurve	Undercurve-to-Overcurve
er ls	ea to	en ly
writer	read	send
e-mails	log on	quickly

Better Letters

Keep your loops open. Write:
e not *i*   *l* not *t*

Use your best handwriting to write the letters again.

Size
Circle your best short letter and your best tall letter.

27

Grade 4 Student Edition page

Students are reminded to focus on the **Keys to Legibility** throughout the year so that Shape, Size, Spacing, and Slant continually improve.

Review activities for all upper- and lowercase letters and numerals reinforce learning and develop automaticity.

Application activities provide writing extension opportunities.

Writing Quickly promotes speed and automaticity so that students can do well in high-pressure testing situations where they must write quickly and maintain legibility.

Zaner-Bloser Handwriting provides options to begin cursive writing instruction in Grade 2 or Grade 3.

The Keys to Legibility

Four Keys to Legibility—**Shape, Size, Spacing,** and **Slant**—are the basis of Zaner-Bloser's unique instructional system. The Keys form an assessment rubric for teachers and students.

Students are introduced to the four Keys at the beginning of the year. As letters are introduced, students self-evaluate the shape, size, spacing, and slant of their handwriting for continual improvement.

Keys are used in the Teacher Edition as prompts for the teacher to remind the students about shape, size, spacing, and slant.

For more information on using the Keys to Legibility to evaluate your students' handwriting, go to **www. zaner-bloser.com/evaluate**.

Consistent terminology, such as the names of the guidelines and the Keys, appears throughout the Student Edition and across all grades.

Grade 4 Student Edition page

Shaping Effective Communicators

Z10

Self-Evaluation for Increased Legibility and Learning

Simple strokes described in academic language are easy to self-evaluate.

Basic Strokes

Undercurve
An **undercurve** is one of the basic strokes used to write cursive letters. An undercurve stroke swings up.

Find an undercurve stroke at the beginning of each letter. Write the letters.

b e h j p t w

B G L P R S

Downcurve
A **downcurve** is one of the basic strokes used to write cursive letters. A downcurve stroke dives down.

Find the downcurve stroke at the beginning of each letter. Write the letters.

a c d g o q

A C D E O

14

Grade 4 Student Edition page

Stop and Check signs throughout the lessons remind students to self-evaluate.

Self-evaluation is an important part of the handwriting process. By identifying their own strengths and weaknesses, students become independent learners.

As students practice, evaluate, and improve their writing, they realize the value of self-evaluation in all of their written work.

Self-Evaluation as Self-Regulation
Self-regulation is a metacognitive process that allows students to monitor their own behavior. It is a valuable skill that predicts academic success and makes all learning possible. The self-evaluation process in this program strengthens students' ability to self-regulate as they practice writing.

Teacher Edition

Confidently teach handwriting in 15 minutes per day with the easy-to-use Teacher Edition.

The three-step lesson presents a clear, simple instructional plan—Model, Practice, Evaluate—and includes

- step-by-step instructions for a wide variety of activities to make teaching handwriting fun and easy.

- embedded professional development to help teachers meet the needs of all students.

- many opportunities to differentiate instruction.

Zaner-Bloser Handwriting works with any language arts curriculum to fully support reading and writing instruction.

Clearly stated objectives guide instruction.

Short, **clear stroke descriptions** use academic language and give teachers the exact words to use when modeling. Teachers have the option of using the detailed stroke descriptions on page T116.

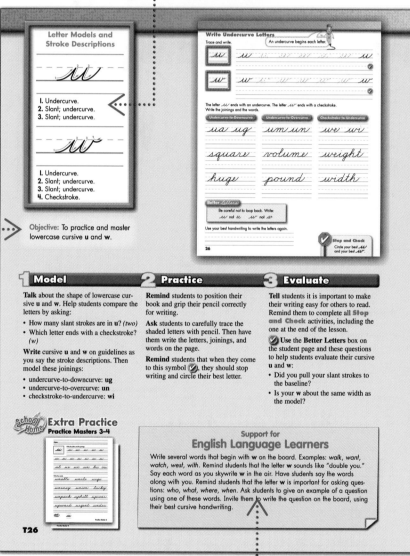

Grade 4 Teacher Edition page

Support for English Language Learners provides the teacher with cultural notes and activities appropriate for students at varying levels of language acquisition.

Shaping Effective Communicators

Z12

Differentiating Instruction

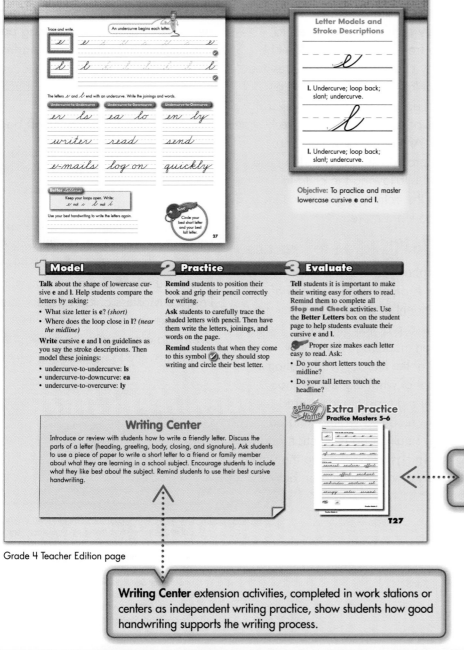

Grade 4 Teacher Edition page

The Teacher Edition provides many opportunities to differentiate instruction:

- **Support for English Language Learners**
- **Tips From an Occupational Therapist**
- **Multisensory activities**

Differentiation can be accomplished both in whole-group instruction and in work stations or learning centers. For more information on using work stations and learning centers, see page Z14.

By explicitly teaching all students in the correct developmental sequence and by differentiating for students' specific needs, all students progress. This reduces the need for costly handwriting-related occupational therapy.

See pages Z18–Z21 for more information on how to meet the needs of all students.

Practice Masters allow the teacher to match additional practice to students' needs.

Writing Center extension activities, completed in work stations or centers as independent writing practice, show students how good handwriting supports the writing process.

Using Work Stations in Your Classroom

By Debbie Diller

Excerpted From *Literacy Work Stations: Making Centers Work* by Debbie Diller

What Is a Work Station?

A literacy work station is an area within the classroom where students work alone or interact with one another, using instructional materials to explore and expand their literacy. It is a place where a variety of activities reinforces and/or extends learning, often without the assistance of the classroom teacher. It is a time for children to practice reading, writing, speaking, listening, and working with letters and words.

Instructional Materials

Instructional materials already used in teaching go into the work stations. The idea is for the teacher to model how to use the materials first, using them with the students to be sure they understand how to use them, then moving these materials into the work stations for independent practice.

A Variety of Activities

Choice is an important feature in making literacy work stations successful. A station should include a variety of things for children to choose from, but there shouldn't be so many choices that the children feel overwhelmed. Aim for what I call "controlled choice." Provide several choices of activities within a work station. Any of the activities there should provide the practice the child needs, but allowing the child to choose the activity will enable him or her to learn more.

Time for Children to Practice

The emphasis at literacy work stations is on practice—meaningful, independent practice. It is a time for children to practice all that the teacher has been modeling. Thus, activities placed at the literacy work stations grow out of what the teacher has done during read-aloud, shared reading, modeled writing, shared writing, small-group instruction and so on. Things aren't put into the work stations just to keep children busy.

The Handwriting Work Station

Materials you may wish to include at your handwriting work station include a variety of writing implements (pencils, pens, crayons, markers), writing paper, and handwriting posters demonstrating proper letter formation. If available, you may also wish to include Touch and Trace Cards™, magnetic letters, and a write-on, wipe-off board.

After each letter has been modeled, students can use the handwriting work station to practice writing letters in various media and choose "my best letter," teach a partner how to make a letter, and trace a letter multiple times in different colors to make a rainbow letter. You might also copy appropriate Practice Masters onto transparencies and make these available at the overhead along with dry erase pens to add novelty to handwriting practice.

Debbie Diller holds a master's degree from Temple University. In her experiences as a classroom teacher, Title I reading specialist, migrant education teacher, literacy coach, national consultant, and author, she has acquired a deep understanding of child development and literacy development, which she uses to address the differentiated needs of students. She is the author of *Spaces & Places, Making the Most of Small Groups, Literacy Work Stations: Making Centers Work,* and *Practice With Purpose.*

Zaner-Bloser
Handwriting
Shaping Effective Communicators

Zaner-Bloser Handwriting promotes automaticity, legibility, and fluency with explicit, systematic handwriting instruction.

"...without direct teaching, the attempt to learn writing often ends in disaster. Any 1st grade child can find and lock onto endless inefficient ways of scribbling around the same letter. Many cases of apparent dysgraphia are the result of inadequate teaching."

—Betty Sheffield, *Handwriting: A Neglected Cornerstone of Literacy*

Zaner-Bloser Handwriting's vertical manuscript supports early reading and writing development through print awareness and improved letter recognition.

"...[modified italic] manuscript is not only harder to learn than traditional print [vertical manuscript], but [it] creates substantially more letter recognition errors and causes more letter confusion than does the traditional style."

—Debby Kuhl and Peter Dewitz, *The Effect of Handwriting Style on Alphabet Recognition*

Zaner-Bloser Handwriting encourages ongoing literacy growth to improve written communications.

"...there has been a steady accumulation of empirical support for the notion that handwriting plays a central role in allowing the production of high quality written text."

—Carol A. Christensen, *The Critical Role Handwriting Plays in the Ability to Produce High Quality Written Text*

Zaner-Bloser Handwriting reduces the need for handwriting-related intervention.

"One of the first things educators can do to ensure that students with special needs develop good writing skills... is to provide them with formal handwriting instruction."

—Susan M. Cahill, *Where Does Handwriting Fit In? Strategies to Support Academic Achievement*

Research

Research-Supported Handwriting Instruction

Research shows that handwriting is an important foundational literacy skill for reading and writing. Research-supported **Zaner-Bloser Handwriting** is backed by more than 120 years of proven results and gives students important tools they will need to be successful communicators in today's world.

Refer to *Handwriting Research: A Guide to Curriculum Planning* to read these and other handwriting research articles.

Z15

Integrate Technology into the Handwriting Classroom

New! ▶ Digital Resources for Handwriting

engages students with rich multimedia lessons for whole-class instruction. Interactive digital resources include proper pencil and paper positions for right- and left-handed students, letter animations that show how to form each letter, and letter activities.

The letter animations provide professional development support for teachers with limited experience in handwriting instruction.

Compatible with any interactive whiteboard brand (or use a regular screen and LCD projector), Digital Resources for Handwriting provides a fluid, intuitive user experience for teachers and students.

Fun, grade-level appropriate letter activities bring letters to life.

New! Practice Masters

CD-ROM contains all practice pages as PDF files.

New! Teacher Edition eBook

At school or at home, with this interactive Teacher Edition, you can

- navigate from the Table of Contents and turn pages.
- search for keywords.
- save notes and highlighted text.

New! ZB FontsOnline Plus™

Now you can save and edit documents using Zaner-Bloser's manuscript and cursive alphabets. The application provides templates for a variety of documents and includes Spanish characters.

Available at **www.zbfontsonline.com**

Optional Support Materials

A full selection of classroom, multisensory, and optional practice materials provide extra support for teaching handwriting and make learning fun!

A. *New!* Alphabet Wall Strips, Grades K–6

B. *New!* Alphabet Desk Strips, Grades K–4

C. Adhesive Desk Strips, Grades 1–4

D. Wipe-Off Practice Cards—Manuscript and Cursive, Grades K–6

E. *New!* ZB FontsOnline Plus™—Manuscript and Cursive, Grades K–6
(See page Z16 for more information.)

F. Manuscript/Cursive Card Sets, Grades 1–4

G. Home Handwriting Pack, Grades K–4

H. Journals and Blank Books, Grades K–6

I. Paper, Grades K–6

J. Touch and Trace Cards— Manuscript and Cursive—PreK–Grade 3

K. Wikki Stix®

L. On the Road to Writing and Reading for PreKindergarten

M. *New!* Fine Motor Skills Development Kit
(See page Z23 for more information.)

N. Animal Alphabet Cards, Grades K–2

O. Fun With Handwriting

P. *New!* Handwriting Research: A Guide to Curriculum Planning

Q. Evaluation Guides—bound in Teacher Editions and available separately—Grades 1–6

R. Music, Mazes & More CD-ROM—included in the Teacher Edition—Grades K–2
(See page Z20 for more information.)

S. *New!* Poster Super Pack
Also available in Spanish.

T. *New!* Digital Resources for Handwriting
(See page Z16 for more information.)

U. *New!* Practice Masters
Also available in Spanish.

V. Handwriting for Middle School

W. Handwriting Correspondence Course

Handwriting Instruction and English Language Learners

By Bertha Pérez, Ed.D., and Ellen Riojas Clark, Ph.D.

Handwriting is an important communication skill that reinforces reading, spelling, and writing. Because of its foundational nature, this skill is important for all children, including English Language Learners (ELLs).

It is essential to know your students' first language (LI) literacy levels. Students who are literate in their first language can draw upon those literacy concepts and skills as they learn to write English (L2). Even when the writing systems are different, research shows that concepts about the meaning and constancy of letters/symbols and skills, such as alphabet knowledge and phonological awareness, will transfer to another language (Cummins, 1992; Cisero & Royer, 1995).

Handwriting instruction will give ELLs a tool for writing. **Zaner-Bloser Handwriting** and **Zaner-Bloser La escritura** use continuous-stroke vertical manuscript to teach the distinctive shapes and features of letters. This instructional approach will lead to mastery of basic writing skills (manuscript and cursive),

improved letter recognition, and fluency in writing. Learning to write the vertical manuscript—the letters children see in books and environmental print—strengthens the L2 reading-writing connection.

The more a teacher understands the mechanics of English spelling and writing, the more successful their ELL students will be (Kroese, Mather, & Sammons, 2006). Teachers can assist students with LI literacy skills to use those skills to write in English (August & Shanahan, 2008). For example, ELLs who know Spanish or other Roman alphabets can use those letter names and sounds to identify the same letters in English.

English orthography might not be easy for ELLs who use a non-alphabetic system, but teachers can assist students to make the connections (Moats & Tolman, 2008). Some ELLs' LI may be written in a different script (such as Chinese or Arabic) or may be organized from right to left (Cloud, Genesee, & Hamayan, 2009). For these ELLs, use visuals to demonstrate handwriting strokes.

The more students attempt to write in English, the more handwriting practice they will acquire. Visual aids such as graphic organizers can help students generate ideas for writing (Sigueza, 2005). In addition, concrete content and language can also help students understand ideas they may wish to express in their writing. It is important to integrate concrete content and language (Morahan & Clayton, 2003). The use of ELLs' background knowledge as a cultural resource (Gonzalez, Moll, & Amanti, 2005) will anchor their writing to their conceptual learning.

ELLs need time and special techniques to acquire the proper handwriting strokes. Teachers can demonstrate the academic language used to teach handwriting (shape, size, spacing, and slant) through Total Physical Response (TPR) and other second language approaches. As you work with ELL students, implement the following:

- Allow the students to watch you forming the letters. Use visuals to demonstrate proper stroke sequence. Say the stroke sequence aloud as you form the letter.

Shaping Effective Communicators

- Use TPR to describe letter formation. For example, point to your head when referencing the headline on the handwriting grid. Say, "Your **head** is the **top** of your body. The **headline** is the **top** line." Similarly, you can demonstrate strokes with TPR. As you say "Slide right," slide your feet across the floor.

- Ask students to describe and demonstrate the steps in creating the letter, whether in L1 or L2.

- Conclude the lesson by having the students apply the new handwriting skill in a meaningful context.

Finally, as the students practice their handwriting, guide your ELLs

- to access their prior knowledge (Jefferies & Merkley, 2001) about what to write about.

- to write as a class, in pairs, or independently (Morahan & Clayton, 2003).

- to use their native language when necessary.

- to write about what they know.

References

August, D. & Shanahan, T. (Eds.). (2008). *Developing reading and writing in second-language learners.* New York: Routledge.

Cisero, C. & Royer, J. (1995). The development and cross-language transfer of phonological awareness. *Contemporary Educational Psychology, 20*(3), 275–303.

Cloud, N., Genesee, & Hamayan, E. (2009). *Literacy instruction for English language learners: A teacher's guide to research-based practices.* Portsmouth: Heinemann.

Cummins, J. (1992). Bilingualism and second language learning. *Annual Review of Applied Linguistics, 13,* 51–70.

Gonzalez, N., Moll, L., & Amanti, C. (Eds.). (2005). *Funds of knowledge: Theorizing practices in households, communities, and classrooms.* Mahwah, New Jersey: Lawrence Erlbaum Associates.

Jefferies, D., & Merkley, D. (2001). Guidelines for implementing a graphic organizer. *The Reading Teacher, 54*(4), 350–357.

Kroese, J., Mather, N., & Sammons, J. (2006). The relationship between nonword spelling abilities of K–3 teachers and student spelling outcomes. *Learning Disabilities: A Multidisciplinary Journal, 14*(2), 85–89.

Moats, L., & Tolman, C. (2008). *English gets a bad rap!* Retrieved from colorincolorado.org/article/28650.

Morahan, M., & Clayton, C. (2003). *Bilingual students in the elementary classroom: A reference for the practicum student at Boston College Lynch School of Education.* Title III Project ALL, Boston College Lynch School of Education.

Sigueza, T. (2005). *Graphic organizers.* Retrieved from colorincolorado.org/article/13354.

La escritura: Parallel Spanish Handwriting Instruction

New! **La escritura** for Grades K–3 provides parallel instruction to the English program so that Spanish-speaking students with limited English can progress in handwriting, a critical literacy skill, alongside their English-speaking peers.

A parallel **La escritura** Student Edition and a **La escritura** Teacher Guide are available. The Teacher Guide includes reduced student pages and Spanish translations of all objectives, stroke descriptions, and self-evaluation questions.

Spanish posters and Practice Masters are also available.

▶ Bertha Pérez, Ed.D., began her career as a classroom teacher in San Antonio, Texas. Later, she earned her doctorate from the University of Massachusetts at Amherst and served as professor of reading and biliteracy at San José State University, The University of Texas at El Paso, and The University of Texas at San Antonio. As a result of her literacy and biliteracy research, Dr. Pérez has become an authority on biliteracy and assisting English language learners to develop biliteracy.

▶ Ellen Riojas Clark holds a Ph.D. in curriculum and instruction from The University of Texas at Austin. Dr. Clark is a Professor of Bicultural Bilingual Studies at The University of Texas at San Antonio. Her research interests include the relationship between the constructs of self-concept, ethnic identity, self-efficacy, and good teaching; bilingual education teacher training; and the identification of gifted language-minority children.

Suggested Activities for Differentiated Instruction

Kinesthetic Learners

- Walk out the letter strokes on the floor.
- Form letters in the air using full arm movement.
- Make letter models with clay, string, or Wikki Stix®.
- Use different writing instruments, such as crayons, markers, and varied sizes of pencils.
- Trace large strokes, letters, and joinings on the board and on paper—first with fingers, then with chalk or other media.

The activities suggested for kinesthetic learners are also appropriate for students who experience attention deficit.

Auditory Learners

- Verbalize each stroke in the letter as that letter is presented.
- Encourage the student to verbalize the letter strokes and to explain how strokes are alike and how they are different in the letterforms.
- Ask students to write each letter as you verbalize the strokes.
- Be consistent in the language you use to describe letters, strokes, shapes, and joinings.

Visual Learners

- Encourage students first to look at the letter as a whole and to ask themselves if the letter is tall or short, fat or skinny. Does all of the letter rest on the baseline, is it a tall letter, or is it a letter with a descender? How many and what kinds of strokes are in the letter?
- Have students look at each individual stroke carefully before they attempt to write the letter.

Music, Mazes & More CD-ROM

Featuring 12 lively sing-along songs, printable song lyrics, and optional practice pages to help students with all learning styles—kinesthetic, auditory, and visual—develop handwriting skills. (Included in Teacher Edition, Grades K–2)

Students With Reversal Tendencies

Directionality

A problem with directionality (moving from left to right across the page) interferes with a student's ability to form letters correctly and to write text that makes sense. To develop correct directionality, try these techniques:

- Provide opportunities for the student to write at the board within a confined area, with frequent arrows as a reminder of left-to-right progression.
- Prepare sheets of paper on which the left edges and the beginning stroke of a letter are colored green.

Letter Reversals

Determine which letters a student reverses most often. Make a list of these reversals and concentrate on them either on an individual basis or by grouping together the students who are reversing the same letters.

- Emphasize each step of the stroke description before the students write a letter.
- Provide a letter for tracing that has been colored according to stroke order. Repeat the stroke description with the students as they write the letter.
- Encourage the students to write the letter as they verbalize the stroke description.

Left-Handed Students

Three important techniques assist the left-handed student in writing.

Paper Position

For manuscript writing, the lower right corner of the paper should point toward the left of the body's midsection. Downstrokes are pulled toward the left elbow.

For cursive writing, the lower right corner of the paper should point toward the body's midsection. Downstrokes are pulled toward the left elbow.

Cursive paper position shown

Pencil Position

The top of the pencil should point toward the left elbow. The pen or pencil should be held at least one inch above the point. This allows students to see what they are writing.

Arm Position

Holding the left arm close to the body and keeping the hand below the line of writing prevents "hooking" the wrist and smearing the writing.

Featured Activity: Skywriting

Skywriting is a technique that allows students to use their large muscles to practice the motor patterns used to form strokes and letters. To skywrite, hold up the index and middle fingers of the writing hand and raise the whole arm.

Students should follow the teacher in forming the featured strokes and letters at a large size in the air. As they skywrite, students should repeat the name of each stroke after the teacher. The teacher should either reverse the motion or turn his or her back so that it is not necessary for students to mirror the teacher's actions.

Kinesthetic learners especially benefit from skywriting to practice a letter's formation before writing it on paper. Auditory and visual learners benefit from teacher modeling of skywriting.

Skywriting is also a great warm-up activity for whole-class handwriting instruction.

A Word About Handwriting

By Jane Case-Smith, Ed.D., OTR/L, BCP, FAOTA

Teachers delight when students demonstrate good handwriting and proudly show their handwriting to peers and parents. Students' success with their first handwritten products is important to building their self-esteem and confidence. For this and many other reasons, learning to write is an important goal of the school curriculum. Teaching children the mechanics of handwriting provides an essential foundation for school success.

The goal of a good handwriting curriculum is to teach children to write letters legibly and efficiently, so that writing becomes fluent and automatic. The program should incorporate evidence-based practices and activities that teach students legible handwriting, including modeling, practice, and self-evaluation. Additionally, the program needs to be developmentally appropriate and include materials and methods that reach students who struggle with handwriting.

Zaner-Bloser Handwriting helps students visualize correct letter formation.
The **Zaner-Bloser Handwriting** Teacher Edition suggests that teachers model letter formation so that students learn the starting point and direction of the stroke. By visualizing how the letter is formed, the student can imitate correct formation and avoid forming bad habits (such as writing letters bottom up).

Zaner-Bloser Handwriting provides the right amount of practice.
The program recommends repeated practice of each letter. Practice is critical to learning any motor skill. Because handwriting is, initially, a motor skill, repeated motor practice using correct letter formation is essential to achieving good handwriting.

Zaner-Bloser Handwriting encourages improvement through self-evaluation.
The Student Edition uses Stop and Checks to remind students to self-evaluate their letter formation. Through self-evaluation, students analyze what they have written and how well it matches the letter model. Once they recognize their best letters, they are more likely to remember how to form the letters correctly. Although the teacher's feedback on letter formation is also important, the student's self-evaluation will have a more enduring effect.

Zaner-Bloser Handwriting uses superior letterforms and strokes.
Researchers have found that simple, continuous handwriting strokes, such as those used in this program, are easiest for children to learn. Vertical manuscript letterforms place minimal demand on motor memory, allowing students to learn handwriting quickly and to focus on other mechanics (such as spelling and grammar) and composing. Zaner-Bloser's four basic manuscript strokes—vertical, horizontal, circle, and slant lines—are easiest for students to learn because they simplify motor planning and visual-motor coordination.

As an occupational therapist, I particularly recommend **Zaner-Bloser Handwriting** for students who struggle with handwriting. The simple continuous stroke vertical manuscript alphabet is easy for at-risk students to learn. The program's use of visual aids and verbal prompts promotes multisensory learning that engages students and supports individual learning styles. The curriculum's emphasis on modeling, practice, and self-evaluation is validated by research that has shown these methods enable struggling writers to become legible, fluent writers.

Zaner-Bloser
Handwriting
Shaping Effective Communicators

Zaner-Bloser Handwriting provides the instruction all students need. Using a formal curriculum to teach handwriting, a foundational literacy skill, has many benefits for students. It is directly related to their attitudes toward and confidence in writing. Good handwriting is linked to improved fluency in writing, improved composition, and higher test scores. In contrast, students who struggle with handwriting often lack confidence in their written work, avoid writing, and become discouraged about expressing their thoughts in written form. Additionally, these students may face barriers to learning across academic areas due to 1) incomplete work because handwriting takes longer, 2) decreased legibility, or 3) short or simple answers because the physical act of writing is too difficult.

It is particularly critical that children who have limitations in prerequisite skills (such as visual motor skills, motor coordination, phonological and print awareness) receive a research-based, well-structured program. Explicit and well-designed handwriting instruction leads to improved legibility, higher quality writing, and positive attitudes toward writing.

Occupational therapists find that when students receive a well-designed handwriting program, such as **Zaner-Bloser Handwriting**, we receive many fewer referrals for our services. Therefore teaching handwriting is cost effective! Most importantly, this program enables students to express their ideas, share their stories with a public audience, and develop enthusiasm for the lifelong skill of writing.

New! **Fine Motor Skills Development Kit**

Promote fine motor skills essential for handwriting with the **Zaner-Bloser Fine Motor Skills Development Kit.**

The kit* includes a Teacher Guide by Mary Benbow, occupational therapist, and the following manipulatives:

- 2 pair of Benbow scissors (1 left-handed and 1 right-handed)
- set of 4 beanbags
- 1 lacing activity
- 1 chalkboard with chalk
- 1 pair of tweezers
- set of 75 linking cubes
- 1 container of red dough and 1 roller
- 1 pair of plastic castanets
- set of 50 double-sided foam counters
- set of 20 plastic chain links
- plastic string

*Contents subject to change

▶ Jane Case-Smith, Ed.D., OT, is professor and director of the Occupational Therapy Division at The Ohio State University. Her research focuses on preschool assessment and school-based interventions. She has completed two outcomes studies examining the effects of school-based occupational therapy services focusing on children's progress in fine motor skills and handwriting. Dr. Case-Smith earned her Ed.D. in curriculum and supervision from the University of Georgia at Athens and her master's in occupational therapy from Western Michigan University in Kalamazoo.

Includes **Teacher Guide** by Mary Benbow

Zaner-Bloser National Handwriting Contest

Legible handwriting is something to be proud of!

Develop, celebrate, and reward legible handwriting—enter the Zaner-Bloser National Handwriting Contest! The annual contest measures the handwriting abilities of students in Grades 1–8 in schools using **Zaner-Bloser Handwriting** materials.

State and national recognition for finalists and schools

National winners for each grade level are selected from state winners. One of the national grade-level winners is selected as the top handwriting student in the country—the Grand National Champion.

About the contest:

- The contest is completely free of charge.
- Over 200,000 students participate each year.
- Entries can be completed in class or at home.
- Entries are judged on shape, size, spacing, and slant.
- Prizes are awarded to students and their teachers and schools.
- Every student earns a Participation Certificate.

20th Anniversary!

For complete contest information and entry materials, call 800.924.9233 or visit www.zaner-bloser.com

Previous Handwriting Contest winners

Zaner-Bloser Handwriting

Shaping Effective Communicators

Z24

Zaner-Bloser

Handwriting

4

ZB **Zaner-Bloser**
The Language Arts and Reading Company

Senior Consultant
Steve Graham, Ed.D., Currey Ingram Professor of Special
Education and Literacy, Vanderbilt University

Occupational Therapy Consultants
Jane Case-Smith, Ed.D., OTR/L, FAOTA, Chair of the
Occupational Therapy Division, Ohio State University
Mary Benbow, M.S., OTR, La Jolla, CA
Asha Asher, MA OTR/L, FAOTA, M.Ed. (Special Education),
Cincinnati, OH
North Shore Pediatric Therapy

ELL Consultants
Ellen Riojas Clark, Ph.D., Professor of Bicultural-Bilingual
Studies, University of Texas at San Antonio
Bertha Pérez, Ed.D., Professor Emeritus of Literacy,
University of Texas at San Antonio

Consultant
Debbie Diller, Educational Consultant, Houston, TX

Occupational Therapy Advisory Board
Kathleen A. Benton-Sanchez, M.P.A., OTR/L, Nashville, TN
Sherry Eisenbach, OT/L, Portland, OR
Elizabeth Gerich, OTR/L, Plymouth, MN
Sheila Martins, OTR/L, North Las Vegas, NV

Carol Miller, OTR/L, Marietta, OH
Leslie N. Parker, OTR/L, Huntington, WV
Tricia Shibuya, OTR/L, Las Vegas, NV
Denaysa Sisemore, M.S., OTR/L, Windsor, CO
Cheryl Weaver, CAS, M.S.Ed., OTR/L, Macedon, NY

Reviewers
Amy Bass, National Heritage Academies, Byron Center, MI
Donetta S. Brown, Birmingham City Schools, AL
Kelly Caravelli, Poway Unified School District, San Diego, CA
Michelle Corsi, East Windsor Regional Schools, NJ
Naomi Drewitz, East Windsor Regional Schools, NJ
Shan Glandon, Tulsa, OK
Karen Jackson, School District of Philadelphia, PA
Liz Knowles, Ed.D., 21st Century Curriculum Designs, LLC,
Del Ray Beach, FL
Rita Olsen, Chicago Public Schools, IL
Geraldine A. Pappas, Detroit Public Schools, MI
Michael E. Pizzingrillo, Roman Catholic Diocese of
Brooklyn, NY
Deborah C. Thomas, Ed.D., Montgomery Public Schools, AL
Ellen Lerch Thomsen, Roanoke County Public Schools, VA
Iefay Williams, School District of Philadelphia, PA

Credits
Art: Shel Silverstein: 8, 86; John Hovell: 17–19, 51, 102,
103, 104, 105, 110; Gary Krejca/Wilkinson Studios: 63, 73;
Tom Leonard: 102
Literature: "It's Dark in Here" from *Where the Sidewalk Ends*
by Shel Silverstein. Copyright © 1974 by Evil Eye Music, Inc.;
"Something Told the Wild Geese" by Rachel Field. Reprinted with the
permission of Atheneum Books for Young Readers, an imprint of Simon
& Schuster Children's Publishing division from POEMS by Rachel Field.
Copyright 1934 Macmillan Publishing Company; copyright renewed ©
1962 Arthur Pederson.; "Ring Around the World" by Annette Wynne,
from *All Through the Year* by Annette Wynne. ©1932 by Annette Wynne.
Published by HarperCollins Publishers. All rights reserved.; "April Rain
Song" by Langston Hughes, from *The Collected Poems of Langston
Hughes*, by Langston Hughes. ©1994 by The Estate of Langston Hughes,
Alfred A. Knopf, a division of Random House, Inc. Published by Random
House, Inc. All rights reserved.; "Keep a Poem in Your Pocket" From
SOMETHING SPECIAL by Beatrice Schenk de Regniers. Copyright 1958,
1986. Used by permission of Marian Reiner.

Photos: moodboard/Corbis: Cover; ©iStockphoto.com/
stepanjezek: 4, 40; ©iStockphoto.com/EcoPic: 4, 46;
©iStockphoto.com/jasanttiso: 4, 69; George C. Anderson
Photography, Inc.: 5, 12–16, 19, 22, 56; ©iStockphoto.com/
sharply_done: 6–7; ©Corbis/SuperStock: 20–21; ©Corbis/Getty
Images: 28; ©iStockphoto.com/asterix0597: 29; ©iStockphoto.
com/kassandra: 35; ©iStockphoto.com/stephenmeese: 41 (jaguar);
©iStockphoto.com/stephenmeese: 41 (toucan); ©iStockphoto.com/
sacco: 41 (anaconda); ©Juice Images/Alamy: 42; ©Mauritius /
SuperStock: 47; ©David Young-Wolff/PhotoEdit Inc.: 48; ©Ed
Bock/Photolibrary: 54–55; ©Henry Brown/Alamy: 62; ©Russell
Burden/Photolibrary: 68; ©Jim Wehtje/Getty Images: 72; ©louis
wulff/Alamy: 76; ©Comstock/Jupiterimages: 80; ©ASSOCIATED
PRESS: 82; ©LWA-Dann Tardif/Corbis: 88–89; ©MARKA/Alamy:
95; ©iStockphoto.com/mpruitt: 96; ©Mark Poloff/Photolibrary:
98; ©iStockphoto.com/Bluberries: 106; ©Gordon McGregor/
Alamy: 108

ISBN: 978-0-7367-6840-5

10 11 12 13 14 997 5 4 3 2 1

Copyright © 2012 Zaner-Bloser, Inc.

All rights reserved. No part of this book may be reproduced or transmitted in any form or by any means, electronic or mechanical, including
photocopying, recording, or by any information storage and retrieval system, without permission in writing from the Publisher. The Publisher
has made every effort to trace the ownership of all copyrighted material and to secure the necessary permissions to reprint these selections. In
the event of any question arising as to the use of any material, the Publisher, while expressing regret for any inadvertent error, will be happy to
make any necessary corrections.
Zaner-Bloser, Inc., P.O. Box 16764, Columbus, Ohio 43216-6764
1-800-421-3018
www.zaner-bloser.com
Printed in the United States of America

Certified Chain of Custody
Promoting Sustainable
Forest Management
www.sfiprogram.org

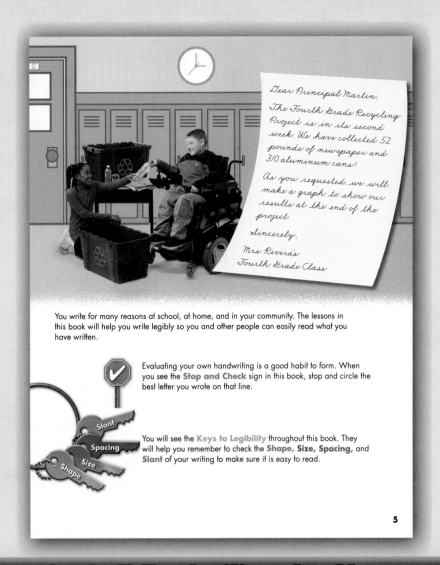

Dear Principal Martin,

The Fourth Grade Recycling Project is in its second week. We have collected 52 pounds of newspaper and 310 aluminum cans!

As you requested, we will make a graph to show our results at the end of the project.

Sincerely,

Mrs. Rivera's Fourth Grade Class

You write for many reasons at school, at home, and in your community. The lessons in this book will help you write legibly so you and other people can easily read what you have written.

Evaluating your own handwriting is a good habit to form. When you see the **Stop and Check** sign in this book, stop and circle the best letter you wrote on that line.

You will see the **Keys to Legibility** throughout this book. They will help you remember to check the **Shape, Size, Spacing,** and **Slant** of your writing to make sure it is easy to read.

5

Grade 4 Handwriting at a Glance

The goal of *Zaner-Bloser Handwriting* is to teach students to write legibly. As you work through the pages of this book with students, you will be helping them learn to write letters, words, and sentences that are legible to both writers and readers. By learning and applying the four Keys to Legibility—**Shape, Size, Spacing, and Slant**—students will evaluate their writing and discover techniques to help them improve and refine their writing skills.

The opening pages are important for laying a foundation for writing. A **Pretest** provides an initial sample of the student's handwriting quality before the year's formal handwriting instruction. **Manuscript Letters and Numerals** and **Cursive Letters and Numerals** present correct models of the forms students will write. **Writing Positions** pages guide students in the correct positions for

sitting, holding the pencil, and positioning the paper. On the pages for **Basic Strokes,** students will become familiar with the lines that form all the letters and numerals in cursive handwriting. The **Keys to Legibility** pages emphasize the qualities of writing that will help students evaluate and improve their handwriting throughout the year.

Writing Lowercase Letters provides practice in writing each lowercase cursive letter. The letters are grouped according to their beginning stroke.

Manuscript Maintenance pages provide an opportunity to review using manuscript writing. On the pages for **Cursive Numerals,** students observe models and write the numerals **1** through **10** with correct strokes.

Writing Uppercase Letters provides practice in writing each uppercase cursive letter, with the letters grouped according to their beginning stroke.

In **Using What You Have Learned,** students have a variety of opportunities to write in different genres for different audiences. Evaluations focus on smaller letter size on new guidelines. **Writing Quickly** and **Writing Easily** enable students to increase their speed and fluency as they gain automaticity in handwriting. Finally, **Handwriting and the Writing Process** helps students review and follow the steps in the writing process as they produce an original piece of writing.

Suggest that students keep a notebook or folder of the writing they do for themselves and for others.

Read student page 5 with your class as an introduction to the *Zaner-Bloser Handwriting* program. Point out to students the features in this book that will help them improve their handwriting.

T5

Background Information

Geese migrate from cooler climates in the north to warmer climates in the south every fall. They must migrate before winter arrives because they feed on vegetation (plants). After cold weather arrives, their food sources will die off or get covered with snow. Likewise, water sources such as rivers and lakes will freeze over.

Objective: To read a poem and discuss its meaning.

Something Told the Wild Geese

Something told the wild geese
   It was time to go.
Though the fields lay golden
   Something whispered,—"Snow."
Leaves were green and stirring,
   Berries, luster-glossed.
But beneath warm feathers
   Something cautioned,—"Frost."
All the sagging orchards
   Steamed with amber spice,
But each wild breast stiffened
   At remembered ice.
Something told the wild geese
   It was time to fly,—
Summer sun was on their wings,
   Winter in their cry.

Rachel Field

6

7

Questions for Discussion

1. What season is occurring in the poem? *(autumn)*

2. What does *luster-glossed* mean? *(having a shiny coating)*

3. Which words in the poem appeal to the reader's sense of sight?

4. Which words in the poem appeal to the reader's sense of touch?

5. Why do you think the poet repeated certain words and phrases in the poem?

Writing Extension

Ask students to write a short paragraph about why wild geese and other birds migrate. Have them provide an explanation for why some species of birds might migrate while others do not.

Before Writing

Point out the poem by Shel Silverstein on student page 8, and read it aloud with students. Tell them that Silverstein was an American writer who lived from 1932–1999. He wrote many cartoons, songs, and poetry for children as well as for adults.

Objective: To demonstrate and assess cursive handwriting.

It's Dark in Here

I am writing these poems
From inside a lion,
And it's rather dark in here.
So please excuse the handwriting
Which may not be too clear.
But this afternoon by the lion's cage
I'm afraid I got too near.
And I'm writing these lines
From inside a lion,
And it's rather dark in here.

by Shel Silverstein

8

Handwriting Coach

Right Hand/Left Hand

To increase awareness of left-handedness, explain that left-handers make up 10–15 percent of the population. Famous "lefties" include Barack Obama, Benjamin Franklin, Albert Einstein, Oprah Winfrey, soccer star Pelé, and baseball stars Sandy Koufax and Babe Ruth. In some sports (baseball, for example), left-handedness is considered to be an advantage.

1 Present the Activity

Explain to students that during handwriting time, they will be writing the letters of the alphabet and the numerals in cursive writing.

Tell students that they will first take a handwriting pretest by writing this poem in their best cursive handwriting. Tell them they will write the poem again at the end of the school year, and then they can compare the writing to evaluate their improvement during the course of instruction and practice.

2 Pretest

Remind students that this pretest will help them evaluate their writing now and later in the school year. Read the poem aloud with students.

Remind students to position their book and grip their pencil correctly for writing. Point out the writing guidelines on student page 9. Then have them write the poem on the page.

Write the poem in your best cursive handwriting.

Is your writing easy to read?   Yes   No

Write your five best cursive letters.

Write five cursive letters you would like to improve.

9

 Evaluate

Monitor and informally assess students' performance as they write. Use this page as a pretest to help you assess each student's current handwriting skills. Then guide them through the self-evaluation process. Meet individually with students to help them assess their handwriting. Ask them how they would like to improve their writing.

Note: Zaner-Bloser's *Evaluation Guide* for Grade 4 handwriting is a useful tool for evaluating students' writing. The evaluation criteria are the Keys to Legibility. Samples of students' handwriting, ranging in quality from excellent to poor, provide a helpful comparison for evaluation.

Handwriting Coach

Evaluation

Self-evaluation is an important step in the handwriting process. By identifying their own strengths and weaknesses, students become independent learners. The steps in the self-evaluation process are as follows:

Question Students should ask themselves questions such as these: "Is my slant correct?" "Do my letters rest on the baseline?" Teacher modeling is vital in teaching effective questioning techniques.

Compare Students should compare their handwriting to correct models.

Evaluate Students should determine strengths and weaknesses in their handwriting based on the Keys to Legibility.

Diagnose Students should diagnose the cause of any difficulties. Possible causes include incorrect paper or pencil position, inconsistent pressure on the writing implement, and incorrect strokes.

Improve Self-evaluation should include a means of improvement through additional instruction and continued practice.

T9

Manuscript Letters and Numerals

Objective: To review manuscript letters and numerals.

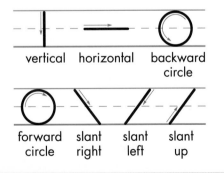

Handwriting Coach

Basic Strokes Practice Practicing the basic strokes at the board is a good method for improving poor strokes for visual and kinesthetic learners. Place sets of two dots to mark the starting and stopping points of each stroke. Invite students to the board, and remind them that the basic strokes, written correctly in specific combinations, yield letters with correct shape.

vertical	horizontal	backward circle

forward circle	slant right	slant left	slant up

1 Review

Have students review the uppercase and lowercase manuscript letters and numerals on student page 10. Remind students that all manuscript letters are formed with four basic strokes—vertical, horizontal, circle, and slant—and that manuscript writing is vertical and not slanted to the right.

Encourage students to use the chart on this page as a resource to review the manuscript letters and numerals.

2 Practice

Have students read the directions and work through the activities on student page 10. Encourage students to write carefully so their writing is legible.

Discuss situations that require manuscript writing to emphasize the need for manuscript. Examples might include job applications, subscription cards, test forms, order forms from catalogs, tax returns, and bank forms.

Discuss potential problems that arise from illegible manuscript writing. If time permits, have students role-play such situations.

Support for English Language Learners

Students who are new to this country might not understand the signs at the bottom of student page 10. Duplicate the signs and include illustrations to communicate their meanings. Point to the illustrations as you read aloud the words on each sign. Use gestures and pantomime to help students understand *Come In* and *Please Knock*. Discuss actions students should take when they see signs such as these.

T10

Cursive Letters and Numerals

Aa Bb Cc Dd Ee Ff Gg
Hh Ii Jj Kk Ll Mm
Nn Oo Pp Qq Rr Ss Tt
Uu Vv Ww Xx Yy Zz
1 2 3 4 5 6 7 8 9 10

Use your best cursive to write the following.

1. Write your name.

2. Write the name of your school.

3. Write the numerals from 1 to 10.

4. Write the lowercase letters you think you use most.

5. Write the letters and numerals you want to improve.

11

Cursive Letters and Numerals

Objective: To review cursive letters and numerals.

1 Review

Review the uppercase and lowercase cursive letters and numerals on student page 11.

Encourage students to use the chart on this page as a resource to review the cursive letters and numerals.

2 Practice

Ask students to read the directions and work through the activities on the page. Encourage students to write carefully so their writing is legible.

Discuss with students how legible writing is crucial for effective communication. Poll students to find out which letters and numerals are most difficult for them to write. Encourage discussion about why they think so.

Encourage activities that offer meaningful handwriting practice, such as friendly letters, jokes and riddles, nametags or labels, charts, vocabulary cards, and simple stories or poems.

Handwriting Coach

Guidelines Review with students the use of guidelines for correct letter formation. Draw guidelines on the board using colored chalk or markers. Identify the headline, the midline, the baseline, and the descender space. Invite volunteers to write words on the guidelines, paying close attention to the size of their letters.

Content Connection   Language Arts

Have students create a writing folder or portfolio. As they progress in their handwriting, they should look through their folders or other school papers and select a sample that best showcases their ability to write legibly. Students might change their selections as their handwriting skills improve.

Objective: To review correct positions for cursive writing.

Left-Handed Writers

Sit like this.
Sit comfortably.
Lean forward a little.
Keep your feet flat on the floor.

Place the paper like this.

Slant the paper as shown in the picture.

Rest both arms on the desk. Use your right hand to shift the paper as you write.

Pull the pencil toward your left elbow when you write.

Hold the pencil like this.

Hold the pencil with your thumb and first two fingers.

Keep your first finger on top.

Bend your thumb and keep it on the side.

Do not squeeze the pencil when you write.

12

Writing Positions

Sitting Position

Using correct body position when writing will help students write better letters. They will also not tire as quickly. Encourage them to sit comfortably erect with their feet flat on the floor and their hips touching the back of the chair. Both arms should rest on the desk. Be sure students are relaxed and are holding their pencil correctly.

Paper Position

Correct paper placement is a critical factor in legibility. To ensure the paper is placed correctly for both right- and left-handed students, use tape to form a frame on the desk so students will be able to place the paper in the correct position.

Left-Handed Writers

Right-Handed Writers

Pencil Position

Model good pencil position for students. The pencil is held between the thumb and the first two fingers, about an inch above the point. The first finger rests on top of the pencil. The end of the bent thumb is placed against the pencil to hold it high in the hand near the knuckle.

Left-Handed Writers **Right-Handed Writers**

Right-Handed Writers

Sit like this.
Sit comfortably.
Lean forward a little.
Keep your feet flat on the floor.

Place the paper like this.

Slant the paper as shown in the picture.

Rest both arms on the desk. Use your left hand to shift the paper as you write.

Pull the pencil toward the middle of your body when you write.

Hold the pencil like this.

Hold the pencil with your thumb and first two fingers.

Keep your first finger on top.

Bend your thumb and keep it on the side.

Do not squeeze the pencil when you write.

13

Writing Positions

Hand Position

The Zaner-Bloser *Writing Frame* can be used to show good hand position for both left-handed and right-handed writers because the hand holding the pencil and resting over the frame automatically settles into the correct position.

Pencil Position

Many students hold their pencils too close to the point. To help students position their fingers on the pencil, demonstrate how to wrap a rubber band tightly around the pencil at least an inch away from the point. Explain that the rubber band shows where to hold the pencil and keeps the fingers from slipping.

Alternative Pencil Position

Students who have difficulty with the traditional pencil position may prefer the alternative method of holding the pencil between the first and second fingers.

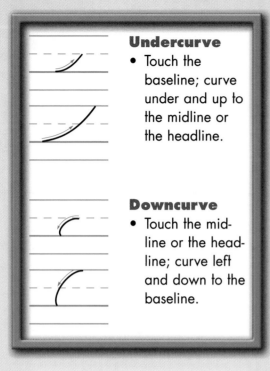

Undercurve
- Touch the baseline; curve under and up to the midline or the headline.

Downcurve
- Touch the midline or the headline; curve left and down to the baseline.

Objective: To practice writing letters with beginning undercurve and downcurve strokes.

Basic Strokes

Undercurve
An **undercurve** is one of the basic strokes used to write cursive letters. An undercurve stroke swings up.

Find an undercurve stroke at the beginning of each letter. Write the letters.

$b \quad e \quad h \quad j \quad p \quad t \quad w$

$B \quad G \quad L \quad P \quad R \quad S$

Downcurve
A **downcurve** is one of the basic strokes used to write cursive letters. A downcurve stroke dives down.

Find the downcurve stroke at the beginning of each letter. Write the letters.

$a \quad c \quad d \quad g \quad o \quad q$

$A \quad C \quad D \quad E \quad O$

14

---

1 Model

Direct students to look at the stroke models and the photos on student page 14. Explain that there are four basic strokes used in forming cursive letters. The undercurve and the downcurve are two of them.

Say the undercurve stroke description. Use skywriting (see Appendix) to model the undercurve stroke in the air. Have students stand and say it with you as they write the undercurve stroke in the air. Then repeat the process with the downcurve stroke description.

Ask students to use their index finger to trace the undercurve and downcurve strokes several times in their book.

2 Practice

Remind students to position their book and grip their pencil correctly for writing.

Ask students to read the directions and write the letters on student page 14. Remind them to begin each letter at the correct starting place. If any students have difficulty identifying the stroke in a certain letter, model the letter on the board and highlight the target stroke in a different color.

Remind students that when they come to this symbol ✅, they should stop writing and circle their best undercurve and downcurve letters.

3 Evaluate

Tell students it is important to make their writing easy for others to read. Remind them to complete all **Stop and Check** activities.

✅ **Use** these questions to help students evaluate their writing:
- Did you begin each letter at the correct starting point?
- Did you end each short undercurve stroke near the midline?
- Did you end each tall undercurve stroke near the headline?
- Did you begin each downcurve stroke at the midline (or at the headline)?

Support for
English Language Learners

Some students might need additional help understanding the words describing the four basic strokes. Provide students with card stock or other heavy paper to cut out the basic strokes that make up a letter. Have them put the parts together to form the letter while saying the name of each stroke.

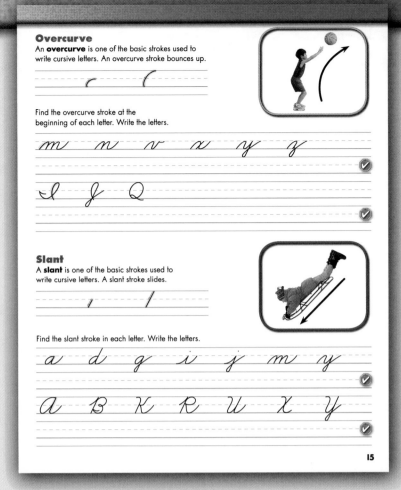

Overcurve

An **overcurve** is one of the basic strokes used to write cursive letters. An overcurve stroke bounces up.

Find the overcurve stroke at the beginning of each letter. Write the letters.

m n v x y z

l f Q

Slant

A **slant** is one of the basic strokes used to write cursive letters. A slant stroke slides.

Find the slant stroke in each letter. Write the letters.

a d g i j m y

A B K R U X Y

15

Overcurve

- Touch the baseline; curve up and right to the midline or the headline.

Slant

- Touch the midline or the headline; slant left to the baseline or the headline.

Objective: To practice writing cursive letters with overcurve and slant strokes.

1 Model

Direct students to look at the stroke models and the photos on student page 15. Explain that the overcurve and the slant are the other basic strokes used to write cursive letters.

Say the overcurve stroke description. Use skywriting to model the overcurve stroke in the air. Have students stand and say it with you as they write the overcurve stroke in the air. Then repeat with the slant stroke description.

Ask students to use their index finger to trace the overcurve and slant strokes several times in their book.

2 Practice

Remind students to position their book and grip their pencil correctly for writing.

Have students read the directions and work through the activities on the page. Remind them to begin each letter at the correct starting place. If any students have difficulty identifying the stroke in a certain letter, model the letter on the board and highlight the target stroke in a different color.

Remind students that when they come to this symbol ✓, they should stop writing and circle their best overcurve and slant letters.

3 Evaluate

Tell students it is important to make their writing easy for others to read. Remind them to complete all **Stop and Check** activities.

✓ **Use** these questions to help students evaluate their writing:

- Did you begin each overcurve stroke near the baseline?
- Did you end each short overcurve stroke near the midline?
- Does each of your tall overcurve strokes end near the headline?
- Do your slant strokes begin at the midline (or at the headline)?
- Do your slant strokes end near the baseline?

Tips From an
Occupational Therapist

Provide each student with sheets of newspaper and a dark crayon or marker. Let students tape their newspapers sideways to the board or wall and use the horizontal columns of type as a large grid. Have them practice their strokes in large, sweeping motions. Encourage them to practice each stroke several times and to feel the motion that each one involves.

T15

Keys to Legibility

Objective: To practice the Shape and Size **Keys to Legibility**.

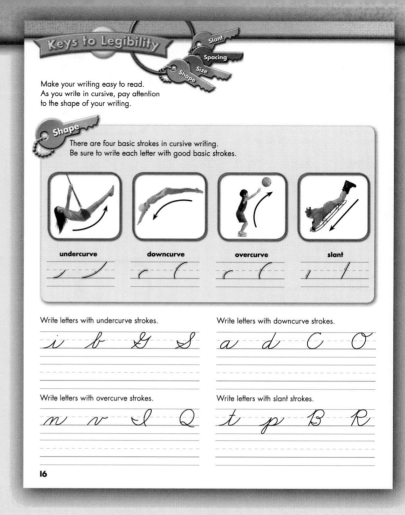

Keys to Legibility

Make your writing easy to read. As you write in cursive, pay attention to the shape of your writing.

Shape

There are four basic strokes in cursive writing. Be sure to write each letter with good basic strokes.

undercurve   downcurve   overcurve   slant

Write letters with undercurve strokes.

i b G S

Write letters with downcurve strokes.

a d C O

Write letters with overcurve strokes.

n v l Q

Write letters with slant strokes.

t p B R

16

Handwriting Coach

Keys to Legibility

Explain to students that good handwriting is legible handwriting. The most important thing to remember is that readers must be able to read a message in order to understand its meaning.

Brainstorm with students qualities of legible handwriting. Write their responses on the board. These might include neatness, carefully written letters, and letters that are not too crowded.

Point out that there are four Keys to Legibility. They are easy to remember because they all start with s: **Shape, Size, Spacing,** and **Slant**.

Explain that **Shape** describes the strokes that form each letter and give it a unique appearance. **Size** describes the height of letters. **Spacing** describes the space between letters, words, and sentences. **Slant** refers to the angle of writing on the paper. Using these Keys will help students improve the legibility of their writing.

1 Present the Key

 Shape

Point out to students that the basic strokes they learned in the previous pages are the basis for a letter's shape.

Read and discuss with students the information and the photographs on student page 16. Then help them as needed as they complete the activities on the page.

2 Practice Shape

Use the overhead projector to project a letter onto the board. Ask students to use a piece of colored chalk or a marker to trace over the stroke you name.

Support for
English Language Learners

To help students understand the meaning of the Keys to Legibility, ask them to prepare a Keys to Legibility booklet to use as a reference throughout the school year. Students can include a page for each Key: Shape, Size, Spacing, and Slant. On the top portion of the page, have students use pictures, photos, and drawings to illustrate the Key. Provide students with magazines and other materials. On the bottom part of the page, ask students to write letters or words as examples of the Keys to Legibility.

T16

Make your writing easy to read.
As you write in cursive, pay attention
to the size of your writing.

Size

Use the guidelines to help you make each letter the correct size.

Tall letters touch the headline.
All uppercase letters are tall.

Short letters touch the midline.

Some letters have descenders
that go below the baseline and
touch the next headline.

Write the tall letters.

Write the short letters.

Write the letters that have descenders.

17

1 Present the Key   ## 2 Practice Size

Size

Read and discuss the information
and illustration on student page 17.
Emphasize that writing letters on
guidelines will help students produce
letters of consistent size. Help students
as needed to complete the activities on
the page. For some students, it may be
helpful to see letter models in a larger
size. Write a few letters on guidelines
on the board. Encourage students to
highlight the headline, midline, and
baseline in different colored chalk or
markers.

Make a set of letter cards by writing
uppercase and lowercase letters in cursive on paper with guidelines. Cut out
each letter and tape it to an index card.
Write **tall** and **short** on the board or
on chart paper to form two columns.
Ask students to select cards and tape
them under the appropriate column.
Model an example for students.

Tall: all uppercase letters, **b, d, f, h,
k, l, t**

**Short: a, c, e, g, i, j, m, n, o, p, q, r,
s, u, v, w, x, y, z**

Ask students to tell how they know
whether letters are tall or short.
Remind them that tall letters touch the
headline and short letters touch the
midline. Invite volunteers to make a
check mark beside cards with letters
that have descenders: **f, g, j, J, p, q, y,
Y, z, Z.**

Support for
English Language Learners

To help students understand the different sizes of letters, have three volunteers
come to the front of the room. Ask one student to stand on a chair (with your
assistance). Have another sit in a chair cross-legged. Have a third student sit in
a chair with one of his or her legs dangling down. Explain that the three positions represent a tall letter, a short letter, and a short letter with a descender.

T17

Keys to Legibility

Objective: To practice the Spacing and Slant **Keys to Legibility**.

Keys to Legibility

Make your writing easy to read. As you write in cursive, pay attention to the spacing of your writing.

Spacing

Between Letters There should be enough space for O.

handwriting

Between Words There should be enough space for \.

between words

Between Sentences There should be enough space for $\circlearrowright$.

Spacing is important. So are shape and size.

Write the sentences. Use correct spacing between letters, words, and sentences.

My writing is neat. It has good spacing.

18

Handwriting Coach

Keys to Legibility

Review the four Keys to Legibility: Shape, Size, Spacing, and Slant. Using these Keys will help students improve the legibility of their writing.

Tell students that Spacing describes the space between letters, words, and sentences. On guidelines on the board, write words, singly or in pairs, with obvious errors in spacing. Challenge volunteers to come to the board, identify an error, and tell how it should be corrected.

Slant refers to the angle of writing on the paper. To help students understand slant, write the same word on the board in cursive and manuscript. Use parallel lines of colored chalk or marker to highlight the difference between manuscript verticality and cursive slant.

1 Present the Key

Spacing

Remind students that good handwriting is legible handwriting. The most important thing to remember is that readers must be able to read a message to understand its meaning. Review that *Spacing* describes the space between letters, words, and sentences. It is a vital part of legibility.

Read and discuss with students the information and illustration on student page 18. Help students as needed to complete the activity on the page.

2 Practice Spacing

Have students find a sample of their cursive writing, and ask them whether they think their spacing helps make their writing easy to read. Ask students to use a colored pencil to draw an o between letters in their words, a \ between words, and an $\circlearrowright$ between sentences. Then ask them to comment on the space between the letters, words, and sentences.

Discuss areas in their writing where spacing is correct and helps make the writing legible and areas where the spacing needs improvement. Finally, ask students to copy several sentences, paying close attention to their spacing.

Support for
English Language Learners

Help students understand Spacing. Stand two hardcover books upright on a desk, close to each other but not touching. Have students describe in words or gestures the amount of space between the books. Tell students that the space between letters in a word is small. Then place the two books farther apart. Tell them they should leave more space between words. Separate the books again, and tell them that there is a larger space between sentences.

T18

Make your writing easy to read. As you write in cursive, pay attention to the slant of your writing.

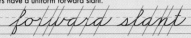

Slant — Cursive letters have a uniform forward slant.

forward slant

 To write with good slant:

POSITION PULL SHIFT

- Check your paper **position**.
- **Pull** your downstrokes in the proper direction.
- **Shift** your paper as you write.

If you are left-handed . . .

Shift your paper as you write.
Pull downstrokes toward your left elbow.

If you are right-handed . . .

Shift your paper as you write. Pull downstrokes toward the middle of your body.

Write the sentence. Check to see if your slant is uniform.

This is good slant.

19

---

1 Present the Key

Slant

Read and discuss the information and the illustrations on student page 19. Emphasize that writing letters and words with uniform forward slant fosters legibility.

Help students as needed to read the directions and complete the activity on the page. Then go over the **Position/ Pull/Shift** information and discuss as needed.

2 Practice Slant

Write the following sentence in cursive on the board: **Slant should be uniform**. Ask a student volunteer to check the slant by using colored chalk or marker to draw lines through the slant strokes of the letters. Then discuss with students whether the slanted lines are parallel to one another. If the lines are not parallel, the slant of the writing is not uniform.

Ask students to write a sentence on a piece of paper with guidelines and then draw lines to check their slant. Help both left-handed and right-handed writers position their paper properly. Remind them to pull their downstrokes in the correct direction and to shift their paper as they write.

Support for
English Language Learners

To help students remember the four basic strokes in cursive writing, present the following verse on an overhead projector or write it on the board.

Undercurves swing. Downcurves dive.
Overcurves bounce. Slants just slide.
Undercurve, downcurve, overcurve, slant.
As you write cursive letters, remember this chant.

Read the verse aloud and have students read it along with you. Encourage students to skywrite the strokes as they read the verse. Have students copy the verse in their best handwriting, applying the four Keys to Legibility.

Background Information

There are many different climates around the world. A Greek scholar named Aristotle developed one of the first systems for grouping the climates. He used three categories: temperate (mild), torrid (hot), and frigid (cold). The groupings were based on distance from the equator. The torrid zones were directly above and below the equator; the frigid zones were near the north and south poles; and the temperate zones were in between.

Objective: To read a poem and discuss its meaning.

Ring Around the World

Ring around the world
Taking hands together
All across the temperate
And the torrid weather.
Past the royal palm-trees
By the ocean sand
Make a ring around the world
Taking each other's hand;
In the valleys, on the hill,
Over the prairie spaces,
There's a ring around the world
Made of children's friendly faces.

Annette Wynne

20

Instructional Manipulatives

Manipulatives in your classroom handwriting center or work station can reinforce and extend your handwriting instruction, especially for kinesthetic learners. Along with a model of the alphabet and a variety of types of paper and writing implements, you might include the following manipulatives to help students practice proper letter and numeral formation.

- Touch and Trace Cards™ Manuscript and Cursive
- Wikki Stix®
- Magnetic Letters
- Write-on, Write-off Magnetic Dry Erase Board

Be sure to model how to use each manipulative before placing it in the handwriting work station. For example, model how to use a Touch and Trace Card with Wikki Stix to form the letter A. See page Z14 for additional work station suggestions.

Questions for Discussion

1. What makes the "ring around the world" in this poem?

2. What parts of the world are described by "palm-trees" and "ocean sand"?

3. Where are the "prairie spaces"?

4. Why might children from different countries get along better than adults from different countries?

5. How do you think the poet feels about children?

Writing Extension

Ask students to work in pairs to list the different climates in the world (according to a current classification, not Aristotle's). Then have them determine which climate they live in and describe its characteristics.

T21

Writing Lowercase Letters

Objective: To practice writing lowercase cursive letters.

Writing Lowercase Letters

To write legibly in cursive, you must form and join lowercase letters correctly. The lessons in this unit will show you how.

As you write, you will focus on shape, size, spacing, and slant to help make your writing legible.

$a \quad b \quad c \quad d \quad e \quad f$

$g \quad h \quad i \quad j \quad k \quad l$

$m \quad n \quad o \quad p \quad q \quad r$

$s \quad t \quad u \quad v \quad w \quad x$

$y \quad z$

Write the lowercase cursive alphabet.

Stop and Check
Circle your three best letters. Underline three letters you want to improve.

22

1 Model

Write the basic strokes on guidelines on the board as you name each stroke. Invite students to say the names as they write the strokes in the air. Point out that lowercase cursive letters are formed with these basic strokes. Then model writing a tall letter, a short letter, and a letter with a descender, noting the placement of each letter on the guidelines. Remind students that all letters of the same size should be the same height.

2 Practice

Remind students to position their book and grip their pencil correctly for writing.

Have students read the information and the directions on student page 22. Then have them write the lowercase cursive alphabet.

3 Evaluate

Tell students it is important to make their writing easy for others to read. Ask them to respond to the evaluation prompt at the bottom of the page.

☑ **Use** these questions to help students evaluate their lowercase cursive letters:

- Did you write with correct strokes so your letters have good shape?
- Do your letters rest on the baseline?
- Do your letters have uniform forward slant?
- Are your short letters half the height of your tall letters?

Support for
English Language Learners

To help students develop a clear mental image of the letter to be written, ask questions about the letter. Model the letter on the board and skywrite it in the air. Ask students to skywrite the letter with you. This will help to establish a visual and motor image.

Beginning Strokes
The lowercase cursive letters are grouped by their beginning strokes.

Undercurve Letters
Trace undercurve strokes.

Trace letters that begin with an undercurve.

Downcurve Letters
Trace downcurve strokes.

Trace letters that begin with a downcurve.

Overcurve Letters
Trace overcurve strokes.

Trace letters that begin with an overcurve.

23

Objective: To practice writing cursive beginning strokes; to practice writing lowercase cursive letters.

1 Model

Point out the lowercase letters on student page 23. Explain that each letter grouping begins with a specific stroke: undercurve, downcurve, or overcurve.

Read aloud each of the letters under each grouping. If necessary, review the description for each stroke.

Ask students to use their index finger to trace the beginning strokes several times in their book.

2 Practice

Remind students to position their book and grip their pencil correctly for writing.

Ask students to trace the beginning strokes and then the letters in each section on student page 23.

Encourage students to summarize what they notice about the strokes and letters on the page in relation to the Keys to Legibility, especially Shape, Size, and Slant.

3 Evaluate

Tell students it is important to make their writing easy for others to read.

✓ **Use** these questions to help students evaluate their beginning strokes.

- Did you end each short undercurve stroke near the midline?
- Did you end each tall undercurve stroke near the headline?
- Did you begin each downcurve stroke at the midline?
- Did you begin each overcurve stroke near the baseline?

Tips From an
Occupational Therapist

Provide large sheets of construction paper and a marker to each student. Have students tape their paper to the board or wall and practice each of the beginning strokes—undercurve, downcurve, and overcurve—in large, sweeping motions. Encourage them to practice each stroke several times and feel the motion that each one involves.

Joinings

Objective: To practice writing letter joinings.

Joinings

Before you join one letter to another, look at the way the letter ends.

Undercurve Ending

The letter i ends with an undercurve. Look at the ways i may be joined to other letters.

Joining i to:	Write the joinings.
Undercurve Beginning $l \rightarrow il$ **Downcurve Beginning** $g \rightarrow ig$ **Overcurve Beginning** $n \rightarrow in$	*it no le ry*

Overcurve Ending

The letter g ends with an overcurve. Look at the ways g may be joined to other letters.

Joining g to:	Write the joinings.
Undercurve Beginning $e \rightarrow ge$ **Downcurve Beginning** $a \rightarrow ga$ **Overcurve Beginning** $n \rightarrow gn$	*gy je zi ya*

Checkstroke Ending

The letter b ends with a checkstroke. Look at the ways b may be joined to other letters.

Joining b to:	Write the joinings.
Undercurve Beginning $e \rightarrow be$ **Downcurve Beginning** $a \rightarrow ba$ **Overcurve Beginning** $y \rightarrow by$	*bi vy oa wa*

24

Handwriting Coach

Joinings Write the lowercase cursive alphabet on the board and guide students in choosing the letters that complete each category of the chart below:

Undercurve ending letters	Undercurve beginning letters
(a, c, d, e, f, h, i, k, l, m, n, p, q, r, s, t, u, x)	(b, e, f, h, i, j, k, l, p, r, s, t, u, w)
Overcurve ending letters (g, j, y, z)	**Downcurve beginning letters** (a, c, d, g, o, q)
Checkstroke ending letters (b, o, v, w)	**Overcurve beginning letters** (m, n, v, x, y, z)

1 Present Joinings

Tell students that joinings are formed by connecting one letter with another letter. The kind of joining is determined by the ending stroke of the first letter and the beginning stroke of the second letter. Choose several of these joinings and list them on the board:

undercurve-to-undercurve
undercurve-to-downcurve
undercurve-to-overcurve
overcurve-to-undercurve
overcurve-to-downcurve
overcurve-to-overcurve
checkstroke-to-undercurve
checkstroke-to-downcurve
checkstroke-to-overcurve

Have students write letter pairs under each head.

2 Practice Joinings

Read the information on the page aloud. Tell students that they should swing wide on the undercurve-to-undercurve joining. Explain that the undercurve-to-overcurve joining becomes a doublecurve. The doublecurve becomes a part of the following letter. Demonstrate these strategies as needed on the board.

Remind students to position their book and grip their pencil correctly for writing and to consider the Keys to Legibility as they write the joinings on student page 24.

✓ **Use** these questions to help students evaluate their joinings.

- Which of your joinings are good?
- Which of your joinings need improvement?

Support for English Language Learners

Say the word "joining" and have students repeat it. Explain that *to join* means to bring together two or more parts. Give an example to illustrate connecting two parts, such as two links in a chain. Then demonstrate how to connect the end of one letter to the start of another. Model common letter combinations, such as **ch, sh, nt,** and **et,** describing the joining type as you write.

T24

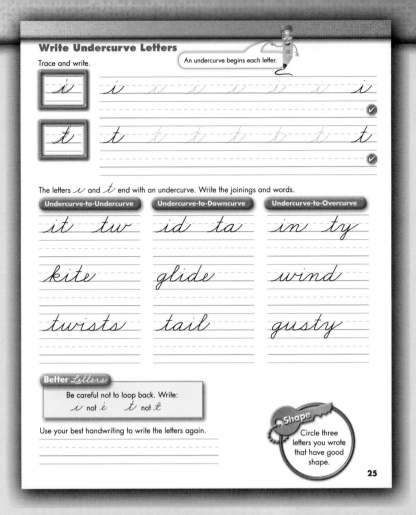

Write Undercurve Letters

Trace and write.

An undercurve begins each letter.

The letters i and t end with an undercurve. Write the joinings and words.

Undercurve-to-Undercurve	Undercurve-to-Downcurve	Undercurve-to-Overcurve
it tw	id ta	in ty
kite	glide	wind
twists	tail	gusty

Better Letters

Be careful not to loop back. Write:

i not e t not l

Use your best handwriting to write the letters again.

Shape Circle three letters you wrote that have good shape.

25

Letter Models and Stroke Descriptions

1. Undercurve.
2. Slant, undercurve. Lift.
3. Dot.

1. Undercurve.
2. Slant, undercurve. Lift.
3. Slide right.

Objective: To practice and master lowercase cursive **i** and **t**.

---

1 Model

Talk about the strokes used to form the shape of lowercase cursive **i** and **t**. Help students compare the letters by asking:

- How does **i** end? *(with a dot)*
- How does **t** end? *(with a slide right)*

Write cursive **i** and **t** on guidelines as you say the stroke descriptions. Use skywriting (see Appendix) to model writing **i** and **t** in the air. Have students stand and say the stroke descriptions with you as they write cursive **i** and **t** in the air. Then model these joinings:

- undercurve-to-undercurve: **it**
- undercurve-to-downcurve: **ta**
- undercurve-to-overcurve: **ty**

2 Practice

Remind students to position their book and grip their pencil correctly for writing.

Ask students to carefully trace the shaded letters with pencil. Then have them write the letters, joinings, and words on the page.

Remind students that when they come to this symbol, they should stop writing and circle their best letter.

3 Evaluate

Tell students it is important to make their writing easy for others to read. Remind them to complete all **Stop and Check** activities. Use **Better Letters** on the student page to help students evaluate their **i** and **t**.

Proper shape makes each letter easy to read. Ask:

- Did you write with correct strokes so your letters have good shape?
- Did you pull your slant strokes to the baseline?
- Did you remember to dot your **i**?

School Home **Extra Practice**
Practice Masters 1–2

Content Connection **Math**

Have students discuss any experience they have had with kites. Poll students to find out how many have made their own kite. Prepare a tally chart on the board. Ask students to think of the best way to present their data in a graph. Accept reasonable responses. Encourage students to make a graph of the data. Have students write a brief report explaining their graph. Remind them to use their best cursive handwriting.

Letter Models and Stroke Descriptions

1. Undercurve.
2. Slant; undercurve.
3. Slant; undercurve.

1. Undercurve.
2. Slant; undercurve.
3. Slant; undercurve.
4. Checkstroke.

Objective: To practice and master lowercase cursive **u** and **w**.

Write Undercurve Letters
Trace and write.

An undercurve begins each letter.

The letter u ends with an undercurve. The letter w ends with a checkstroke. Write the joinings and the words.

Undercurve-to-Downcurve	Undercurve-to-Overcurve	Checkstroke-to-Undercurve
ua ug	um un	we wi
square	volume	weight
huge	pound	width

Better Letters

Be careful not to loop back. Write:
u not ee w not ue

Use your best handwriting to write the letters again.

26

Stop and Check
Circle your best u and your best w.

---

1 Model

Talk about the shape of lowercase cursive **u** and **w**. Help students compare the letters by asking:

- How many slant strokes are in **u**? *(two)*
- Which letter ends with a checkstroke? *(w)*

Write cursive **u** and **w** on guidelines as you say the stroke descriptions. Then model these joinings:

- undercurve-to-downcurve: **ug**
- undercurve-to-overcurve: **un**
- checkstroke-to-undercurve: **wi**

2 Practice

Remind students to position their book and grip their pencil correctly for writing.

Ask students to carefully trace the shaded letters with pencil. Then have them write the letters, joinings, and words on the page.

Remind students that when they come to this symbol ✓, they should stop writing and circle their best letter.

3 Evaluate

Tell students it is important to make their writing easy for others to read. Remind them to complete all **Stop and Check** activities, including the one at the end of the lesson.

✓ **Use** the **Better Letters** box on the student page and these questions to help students evaluate their cursive **u** and **w**:

- Did you pull your slant strokes to the baseline?
- Is your **w** about the same width as the model?

School Home Extra Practice
Practice Masters 3–4

Support for
English Language Learners

Write several words that begin with **w** on the board. Examples: *walk, want, watch, west, with*. Remind students that the letter **w** sounds like "double you." Say each word as you skywrite **w** in the air. Have students say the words along with you. Remind students that the letter **w** is important for asking questions: *who, what, where, when*. Ask students to give an example of a question using one of these words. Invite them to write the question on the board, using their best cursive handwriting.

T26

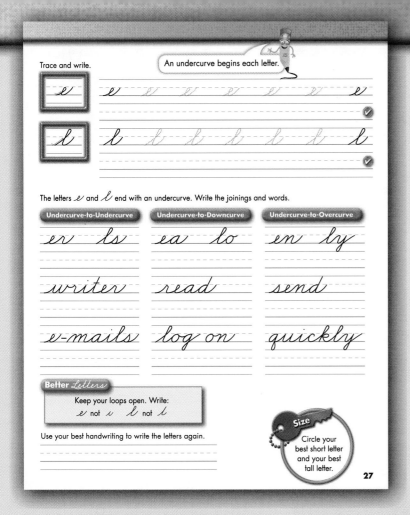

Trace and write.

An undercurve begins each letter.

The letters e and l end with an undercurve. Write the joinings and words.

Undercurve-to-Undercurve	Undercurve-to-Downcurve	Undercurve-to-Overcurve
er ls	ea to	en ly
writer	read	send
e-mails	log on	quickly

Better Letters
Keep your loops open. Write:
e not ι l not l

Use your best handwriting to write the letters again.

Size
Circle your best short letter and your best tall letter.

27

Letter Models and Stroke Descriptions

1. Undercurve; loop back; slant; undercurve.

1. Undercurve; loop back; slant; undercurve.

Objective: To practice and master lowercase cursive **e** and **l**.

1 Model

Talk about the shape of lowercase cursive **e** and **l**. Help students compare the letters by asking:

- What size letter is **e**? (short)
- Where does the loop close in **l**? (near the midline)

Write cursive **e** and **l** on guidelines as you say the stroke descriptions. Then model these joinings:

- undercurve-to-undercurve: **ls**
- undercurve-to-downcurve: **ea**
- undercurve-to-overcurve: **ly**

2 Practice

Remind students to position their book and grip their pencil correctly for writing.

Ask students to carefully trace the shaded letters with pencil. Then have them write the letters, joinings, and words on the page.

Remind students that when they come to this symbol (✓), they should stop writing and circle their best letter.

3 Evaluate

Tell students it is important to make their writing easy for others to read. Remind them to complete all **Stop and Check** activities. Use the **Better Letters** box on the student page to help students evaluate their cursive **e** and **l**.

Proper size makes each letter easy to read. Ask:

- Do your short letters touch the midline?
- Do your tall letters touch the headline?

School Home **Extra Practice**
Practice Masters 5–6

Writing Center

Introduce or review with students how to write a friendly letter. Discuss the parts of a letter (heading, greeting, body, closing, and signature). Ask students to use a piece of paper to write a short letter to a friend or family member about what they are learning in a school subject. Encourage students to include what they like best about the subject. Remind students to use their best cursive handwriting.

Review

Checkstroke Alert

Objective: To review lowercase cursive **i, t, u, w, e,** and **l**; to practice writing the checkstroke joining.

Review

Write the words and the phrases.

inventions

screen   start   link

computer   websites

bulletin board   laptop

printer   file   online

Checkstroke Alert Join *w* and *r* at the midline. Write the joinings and the words.

wr   wr   wr   wr   wr

write   wrist   wrap

28

1 Review

Review the stroke descriptions, and model again any letters the students might be having difficulty writing. Point out that **i, t, u, w, e,** and **l** all begin with an undercurve.

Ask a volunteer to give a verbal description of one of these letters: **i, t, u, w, e, l**. Challenge the other students to identify the letter being described and then write it on guidelines on the board.

See the **Corrective Strategies** in the Appendix for techniques in correcting common prolems in your students' handwriting.

2 Practice

Remind students to position their book and grip their pencil correctly for writing.

Ask students to write the words on the page, remembering to form their letters with correct strokes so they have proper shape. Then have them read and follow the directions for the **Checkstroke Alert** near the bottom of the page.

3 Evaluate

Tell students it is important to make their writing easy for others to read.

✅ **Use** these questions to help students evaluate their cursive writing:

• Did you write with correct strokes so your letters have good shape?

• Do your letters rest on the baseline?

• Do your short letters with descenders touch the headline of the next writing space?

Digital Resources for Handwriting

Interactive digital resources for whole-class instruction include proper pencil and paper positions for right- and left-handed students, letter animations that show how to form each letter, and letter activities. (Interactive whiteboard compatible.)

Support for English Language Learners

Some of the computer terms on student page 28 might be unfamiliar to ELL students. Explain that a *laptop* is a type of *computer* small enough to use on top of your lap. Explain that *web sites* are pages that you view on the computer when you are using the Internet, or you are *online*. A *link* is a chain of words or symbols that takes you to another web site. A link, if you click on it, can also open a *file*, or document. Challenge students to write a sentence that uses all of the Review letters: **i, t, u, w, e,** and **l**. For example: *Bill went to the computer lab.*

T28

Write a paragraph about what you see in the picture.
Use words in the word bank. Be sure to leave space for margins.

hard drive
keyboard
monitor
mouse
mouse pad
power cord
printer
speakers

My writing has good _____ ☐
My writing has good _____ ☐
My writing has good _____ ☐
My writing has good _____ ☐

29

Objective: To write a paragraph with words related to computer components using legible handwriting.

1 Review

Read aloud the words related to computer components on student page 29. If necessary, explain the purpose of each component. Invite volunteers to use a class computer to identify the components of a computer they know and have experience with.

Remind students to correctly form **i, t, u, w, e,** and **l** when they write.

2 Practice

Remind students to position their books and grip their pencils correctly for writing.

Ask students to read the directions and work through the activity on student page 29. Encourage students to write carefully, remembering to form their letters with correctly written strokes so they will have good shape.

3 Evaluate

Tell students it is important to make their writing easy for others to read.

Proper Shape, Size, Spacing, and Slant make words easy to read. Ask:

- Did you write with correct strokes so your letters have good shape?
- Are your letters the correct size?
- Is there proper space between each letter, word, and sentence?
- Does your writing have conistent slant like the model?

Content Connection Technology

Have students use the photo as a model to draw a computer and printer. Have them write the computer-related words and add leader lines to identify the parts of the computer and printer. Encourage students to write a sentence that explains the purpose of each component. Remind students to use their best cursive handwriting.

T29

Letter Models and Stroke Descriptions

1. Undercurve; loop back; slant; undercurve.
2. Checkstroke.

1. Undercurve; loop back; slant.
2. Overcurve; slant; undercurve.

Objective: To practice and master lowercase cursive **b** and **h**.

Write Undercurve Letters

Trace and write.

An undercurve begins each letter.

The letter *b* ends with a checkstroke. The letter *h* ends with an undercurve. Write the joinings and the words.

Checkstroke-to-Undercurve	Checkstroke-to-Downcurve	Undercurve-to-Undercurve
bi br	ba bo	he hu
bike	bars	helmet
brakes	boxcar	hum

Better Letters

Keep your loops open. Write:
b not *b*   *h* not *h*

Use your best handwriting to write the letters again.

30

Stop and Check
Circle your best *b* and your best *h*.

1 Model

Talk about the shape of lowercase cursive **b** and **h**. Help students compare the letters by asking:

• How does **b** end? *(with a checkstroke)*
• What stroke follows the first slant in **h**? *(overcurve)*

Write cursive **b** and **h** on guidelines as you say the stroke descriptions. Then model these joinings:

• checkstroke-to-undercurve: **br**
• checkstroke-to-downcurve: **ba**
• undercurve-to-undercurve: **hu**

2 Practice

Remind students to position their book and grip their pencil correctly for writing.

Ask students to carefully trace the shaded letters with pencil. Then have them write the letters, joinings, and words on the page.

Remind students that when they come to this symbol ✓, they should stop writing and circle their best letter.

3 Evaluate

Tell students it is important to make their writing easy for others to read. Remind them to complete all **Stop and Check** activities, including the one at the end of the lesson.

✓ **Use** the **Better Letters** box on the student page and these questions to help students evaluate their cursive **b** and **h**:

• Does your checkstroke end at the midline?
• Is your **h** about the same width as the model?

School Home Extra Practice
Practice Masters 7–8

Support for
English Language Learners

Students may know that the letter **b** has the /b/ sound as in *ball, bear,* and *bird*. They might not realize that sometimes the sound of the letter **b** is silent, such as when it follows **m,** as in *lamb,* or when it comes before the letter **t,** as in *debt*. Write **ball, bear, debt, lamb,** and **bird** on the board. Point to each word, say it, and have students repeat it after you. Point out for students when the **b** is pronounced and when it is silent.

Trace and write.

An undercurve begins each letter.

The letters f and k end with an undercurve. Write the joinings and words.

Undercurve-to-Undercurve	Undercurve-to-Downcurve	Undercurve-to-Overcurve
fl ks	fo ka	fy ky
flow	foam	leafy
creeks	kayak	risky

Better Letters
Keep your loops open. Write:
f not f k not k

Use your best handwriting to write the letters again.

Spacing — Circle your best joining.

31

Letter Models and Stroke Descriptions

1. Undercurve; loop back; slant; loop forward.
2. Undercurve.

1. Undercurve; loop back; slant.
2. Overcurve; curve forward; curve under.
3. Slant right; undercurve.

Objective: To practice and master lowercase cursive **f** and **k**.

1 Model

Talk about the shape of lowercase cursive **f** and **k**. Help students compare the letters by asking:

- How are **f** and **k** alike? (*Both begin and end with an undercurve; both have a loop that closes near the midline.*)
- Where does the lower loop close in **f**? (*at the baseline*)

Write cursive **f** and **k** on guidelines as you say the stroke descriptions. Then model these joinings:

- undercurve-to-undercurve: **fl**
- undercurve-to-downcurve: **fo**
- undercurve-to-overcurve: **ky**

2 Practice

Remind students to position their book and grip their pencil correctly for writing.

Ask students to carefully trace the shaded letters with pencil. Then have them write the letters, joinings, and words on the page.

Remind students that when they come to this symbol ✓, they should stop writing and circle their best letter.

3 Evaluate

Tell students it is important to make their writing easy for others to read. Remind them to complete all **Stop and Check** activities. Use the **Better Letters** box on the student page to help students evaluate their cursive **f** and **k**.

Proper spacing makes each letter easy to read. Ask:

- Does your writing have good spacing?
- Is there enough space for o between your letters?

School Home Extra Practice
Practice Masters 9–10

Tips From an
Occupational Therapist

Projects involving the use of a ruler force students to use both hands and improve fine-motor skills. Help students make colorful placemats out of different colored construction paper. Have students use a ruler to measure five rectangles, each two inches shorter in length and in width than the previous rectangle. Then have them glue the rectangles one on top of another so that the smallest rectangle is in the middle.

T31

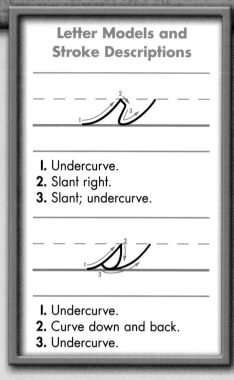

Letter Models and Stroke Descriptions

1. Undercurve.
2. Slant right.
3. Slant; undercurve.

1. Undercurve.
2. Curve down and back.
3. Undercurve.

Objective: To practice and master lowercase cursive **r** and **s**.

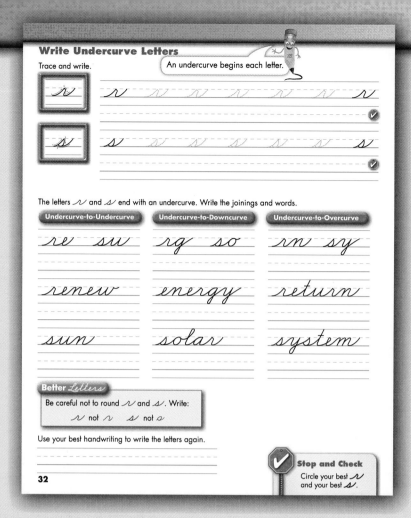

Write Undercurve Letters

Trace and write.

An undercurve begins each letter.

The letters r and s end with an undercurve. Write the joinings and words.

Undercurve-to-Undercurve	Undercurve-to-Downcurve	Undercurve-to-Overcurve
re su	rg so	rn sy
renew	energy	return
sun	solar	system

Better Letters

Be careful not to round r and s. Write:
r not v s not o

Use your best handwriting to write the letters again.

Stop and Check
Circle your best r and your best s.

32

1 Model

Talk about the shape of lowercase cursive **r** and **s**. Ask:

• Which letter has a curve down stroke? *(s)*

• Which has a slant right stroke? *(r)*

Write cursive **r** and **s** on guidelines as you say the stroke descriptions. Then model these joinings:

• undercurve-to-undercurve: **su**
• undercurve-to-downcurve: **rg**
• undercurve-to-overcurve: **sy**

2 Practice

Remind students to position their book and grip their pencil correctly for writing.

Ask students to carefully trace the shaded letters with pencil. Then have them write the letters, joinings, and words on the page.

Remind students that when they come to this symbol, they should stop writing and circle their best letter.

3 Evaluate

Tell students it is important to make their writing easy for others to read. Remind them to complete all **Stop and Check** activities.

Use the **Better Letters** box on the student page and these questions to help students evaluate their cursive **r** and **s**:

• Is the bottom of your **s** closed?

• Does your **r** have good slant?

School Home Extra Practice
Practice Masters 11–12

Support for
English Language Learners

To help students with the /r/ sound, write the words **rain, rule, ranch, radish, wrap, wrote,** and **wrist** on the board. Call attention to the words *wrap, wrote,* and *wrist*. Explain that sometimes the /r/ sound is spelled **wr**. In this spelling, the letter **w** is silent. Say the words, emphasizing the /r/ sound. Then have students say the words with you.

T32

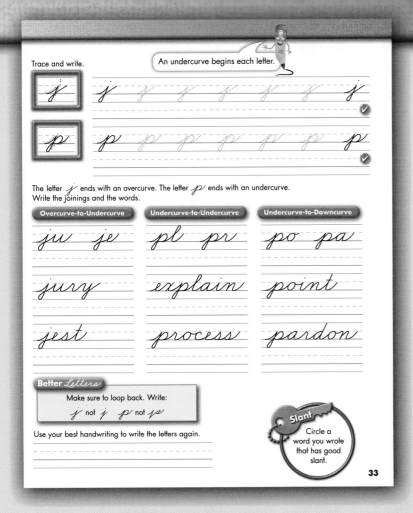

An undercurve begins each letter.

Trace and write.

The letter j ends with an overcurve. The letter p ends with an undercurve.
Write the joinings and the words.

Overcurve-to-Undercurve	Undercurve-to-Undercurve	Undercurve-to-Downcurve
ju je	pl pr	po pa
jury	explain	point
jest	process	pardon

Better *Letters*
Make sure to loop back. Write:
j not j p not p

Use your best handwriting to write the letters again.

Slant
Circle a word you wrote that has good slant.

33

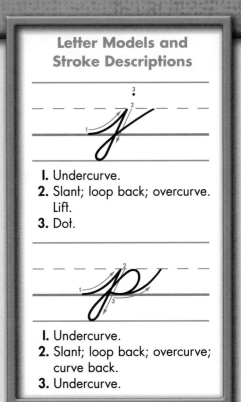

Letter Models and Stroke Descriptions

1. Undercurve.
2. Slant; loop back; overcurve. Lift.
3. Dot.

1. Undercurve.
2. Slant; loop back; overcurve; curve back.
3. Undercurve.

Objective: To practice and master lowercase cursive **j** and **p**.

1 Model

Talk about the shape of lowercase cursive **j** and **p**. Ask:
- Where does the beginning undercurve end in **p**? *(at the midline)*
- How does **j** end? *(with a dot)*

Write cursive **j** and **p** on guidelines as you say the stroke descriptions. Then model these joinings:
- overcurve-to-undercurve: **je**
- undercurve-to-undercurve: **pl**
- undercurve-to-downcurve: **pa**

2 Practice

Remind students to position their book and grip their pencil correctly for writing.

Ask students to carefully trace the shaded letters with pencil. Then have them write the letters, joinings, and words on the page.

Remind students that when they come to this symbol ✅, they should stop writing and circle their best letter.

3 Evaluate

Tell students it is important to make their writing easy for others to read. Remind them to complete all **Stop and Check** activities. Use the **Better Letters** box on the student page to help students evaluate their cursive **j** and **p**.

Proper slant makes each letter easy to read. Ask:
- Do your cursive letters have uniform forward slant?
- Did you pull your downstrokes in the proper direction?

School Home **Extra Practice**
Practice Masters 13–14

Writing Center

Put the **b, h, f, k, r, s, j,** and **p** *Touch and Trace Cards* in the Writing Center so students can check their knowledge of letter formation. For each card, students should follow these steps:
1. Look at the card. Identify the letter and look at the arrow that shows where to begin.
2. Trace the letter with eyes closed. Follow the correct stroke sequence.
3. Check the stroke formation with eyes open.
4. Write the letter on paper, making sure to use correct stroke sequence.

Review

Joining Alert

Objective: To review lowercase cursive **b, h, f, k, r, s, j,** and **p;** to practice writing the undercurve-to-downcurve joining.

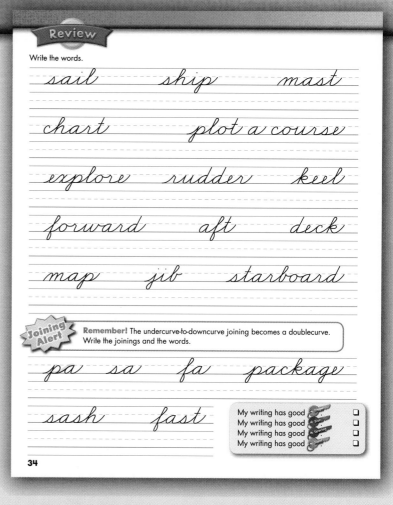

---

1 Review

Review the stroke descriptions, and model any letters students might be having difficulty writing. Point out that the letters **b, h, f, k, r, s, j,** and **p** begin with an undercurve.

Ask a volunteer to give a verbal description of one of these letters: **b, h, f, k, r, s, j, p**. Challenge the other students to identify the letter being described and then write it on guidelines on the board.

See the **Corrective Strategies** in the Appendix for techniques in correcting common problems in your students' handwriting.

Digital Resources for Handwriting

Interactive digital resources for whole-class instruction include proper pencil and paper positions for right- and left-handed students, letter animations that show how to form each letter, and letter activities. (Interactive whiteboard compatible.)

2 Practice

Remind students to position their books and grip their pencils correctly for writing.

Ask students to carefully write the words on the page, remembering to form letters with correct shape. Then have them read and follow the directions for the **Joining Alert** near the bottom of the page.

3 Evaluate

Tell students it is important to make their writing easy for others to read.

Proper Shape, Size, Spacing, and Slant make words easy to read. Ask:

- Did you write with correct strokes so your letters have good shape?
- Did you write letters with good size to fit the writing space?
- Is there proper space between each letter and word?
- Did you maintain uniform forward slant?

Support for
English Language Learners

Some students might need help with multiple-meaning words such as *ship*. Explain that some English words are spelled and pronounced the same but have different meanings. Ask students what they think *ship* means. Explain that a *ship* is a vessel that is larger than a boat and *to ship* means to send a package or cargo by some means of transportation, such as a truck, boat, plane, or train. List other multiple-meaning words and discuss them with students.

T34

Application

Write these sentences about water sports in cursive.
Then answer the question at the bottom of the page.

Gio went sailing.

Jack likes to go fishing.

Kijana loves swimming.

Aiko wants to scuba dive.

What is your favorite water sport? Write a short paragraph in cursive describing what you like to do on or in the water. Remember to indent the first line of the paragraph and leave space for margins.

Stop and Check
Circle your best letter.

35

Application

Objective: To write sentences about watersports using legible handwriting.

1 Review

Read aloud the sentences on student page 35. Review the water sports with the students. Invite volunteers to say what they know about these sports.

Remind students to correctly form **b, h, f, k, r, s, j,** and **p** when they write.

2 Practice

Remind students to position their book and grip their pencil correctly for writing.

Ask students to read the directions and work through the activity on student page 35. Encourage students to write carefully, remembering to form their letters with correctly written strokes so they will have good shape.

Remind students to indent the first line of the paragraph and leave space for margins.

3 Evaluate

Tell students it is important to make their writing easy for others to read. Remind them to complete the **Stop and Check** activity at the end of the lesson.

Use these questions to help students evaluate their writing:
- Did you write with correct strokes so your letters have good shape?
- Did you use the guidelines to make letters with correct size?

Tips From an
Occupational Therapist

Have students build bridges out of toothpicks. Provide them with scissors, glue, cardboard, and small blocks. Have students stack small weights on the completed bridges to see which one can hold the most weight. Manipulating the small toothpicks with their fingertips will build fine-motor skills, and using both hands will promote functional bimanual skills.

Letter Models and Stroke Descriptions

1. Downcurve; undercurve.
2. Slant; undercurve.

1. Downcurve; undercurve.
2. Slant; undercurve.

Objective: To practice and master lowercase cursive **a** and **d**.

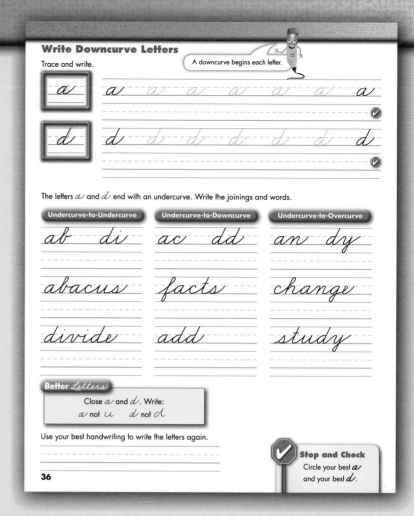

Write Downcurve Letters

Trace and write.

A downcurve begins each letter.

The letters a and d end with an undercurve. Write the joinings and words.

Undercurve-to-Undercurve
ab di
abacus
divide

Undercurve-to-Downcurve
ac dd
facts
add

Undercurve-to-Overcurve
an dy
change
study

Better Letters
Close a and d. Write:
a not u d not cl

Use your best handwriting to write the letters again.

Stop and Check
Circle your best a and your best d.

36

---

1 Model

Talk about the shape of lowercase cursive **a** and **d**. Ask:

- How are **a** and **d** alike? (*They have the same stroke description.*)

Write cursive **a** and **d** on guidelines on the board. Use skywriting (see Appendix) to model writing **a** and **d** in the air.

Ask students to use their index finger to trace cursive **a** and **d** several times in their book. Then model these joinings:

- undercurve-to-undercurve: **ab**
- undercurve-to-downcurve: **dd**
- undercurve-to-overcurve: **an**

2 Practice

Remind students to position their book and grip their pencil correctly for writing.

Ask students to carefully trace the shaded letters with pencil. Then have them write the letters, joinings, and words on the page.

Remind students that when they come to this symbol (✓), they should stop writing and circle their best letter.

3 Evaluate

Tell students it is important to make their writing easy for others to read. Remind them to complete all **Stop and Check** activities, including the one at the end of the lesson.

✓ **Use** the **Better Letters** box on the student page and these questions to help students evaluate their cursive **a** and **d**:

- Is your **a** closed?
- Does the downcurve of your **d** begin at the midline?

School Home Extra Practice
Practice Masters 15–16

Support for English Language Learners

Write sample math problems on the board to help students understand the meaning of such words as *divide, add, facts,* and *change.* Draw simple pictures to illustrate what students are being asked to do in each problem, and have them solve the problems. Have students write each word on a sheet of paper. Then have them use each word in a sentence and draw a picture to help them remember the meaning of the word. Invite students to keep this picture dictionary in their math folder as a reference.

T36

Trace and write.

A downcurve begins each letter.

g g g g g g g

o o o o o o o

The letter g ends with an overcurve. The letter o ends with a checkstroke.
Write the joinings and words.

Overcurve-to-Undercurve

gr ge

$green$

$oxygen$

Checkstroke-to-Undercurve

ob ol

$global$

$ecology$

Checkstroke-to-Overcurve

on oy

one

$enjoy$

Better Letters

Be careful to close g and o. Write:
g not y o not v

Use your best handwriting to write the letters again.

Shape
Circle your three best letters that begin with a downcurve.

37

Letter Models and Stroke Descriptions

1. Downcurve; undercurve.
2. Slant; loop back; overcurve.

1. Downcurve; undercurve.
2. Checkstroke.

Objective: To practice and master lowercase cursive **g** and **o**.

1 Model

Talk about the shape of lowercase cursive **g** and **o**. Ask:

• Where does the loop in **g** close? *(near the baseline)*

• Where does **o** begin? *(just below the midline)*

Write cursive **g** and **o** on guidelines on the board as you say the stroke descriptions. Use skywriting to model writing **g** and **o** in the air. Then model these joinings:

• overcurve-to-undercurve: **gr**
• checkstroke-to-undercurve: **ob**
• checkstroke-to-overcurve: **on**

2 Practice

Remind students to position their book and grip their pencil correctly for writing.

Ask students to carefully trace the shaded letters with pencil. Then have them write the letters, joinings, and words on the page.

Remind students that when they come to this symbol , they should stop writing and circle their best letter.

3 Evaluate

Tell students it is important to make their writing easy for others to read. Remind them to complete all **Stop and Check** activities. Use the **Better Letters** box on the student page to help students evaluate their cusive **g** and **o**.

Proper shape makes each letter easy to read. Ask:

• Do your letters have good shape?

• Does your **o** end with a checkstroke?

School Home **Extra Practice**
Practice Masters 17–18

Content Connection Science

Discuss with students the meanings of the term *green*, other than the color green. Tell them that *green* also means "concerned with or supporting protection of the environment." Have students write a journal entry about ways they work toward protecting the environment each day. Then have students share their writing in a small group.

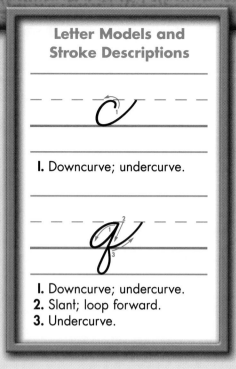

Letter Models and Stroke Descriptions

c

1. Downcurve; undercurve.

q

1. Downcurve; undercurve.
2. Slant; loop forward.
3. Undercurve.

Objective: To practice and master lowercase cursive **c** and **q**.

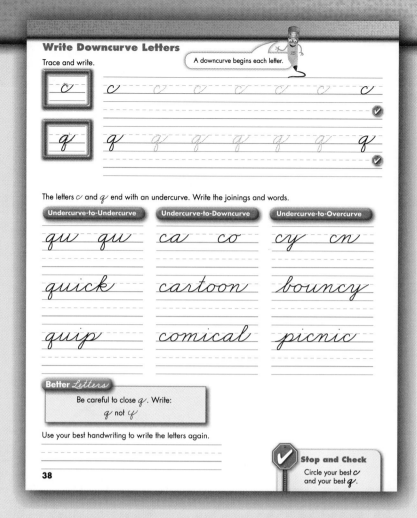

Write Downcurve Letters

Trace and write.

A downcurve begins each letter.

The letters *c* and *q* end with an undercurve. Write the joinings and words.

Undercurve-to-Undercurve

qu qu

quick

quip

Undercurve-to-Downcurve

ca co

cartoon

comical

Undercurve-to-Overcurve

cy cn

bouncy

picnic

Better Letters

Be careful to close *q*. Write: *q* not *y*

Use your best handwriting to write the letters again.

Stop and Check
Circle your best *c* and your best *q*.

38

---

1 Model

Talk about the shape of lowercase cursive **c** and **q**. Help students compare the letters by asking:

- Where does **c** begin? *(below the midline)*
- How does **q** end? *(with an undercurve)*

Write cursive **c** and **q** on guidelines on the board. Then model these joinings:

- undercurve-to-undercurve: **qu**
- undercurve-to-downcurve: **co**
- undercurve-to-overcurve: **cy**

2 Practice

Remind students to position their book and grip their pencil correctly for writing.

Ask students to carefully trace the shaded letters with pencil. Then have them write the letters, joinings, and words on the page.

Remind students that when they come to this symbol ✓, they should stop writing and circle their best letter.

3 Evaluate

Tell students it is important to make their writing easy for others to read. Remind them to complete all **Stop and Check** activities, including the one at the end of the lesson.

✓ Use the **Better Letters** box on the student page and these questions to help students evaluate their cursive **c** and **q**:

- Does your **c** begin below the midline?
- Does your **q** have good slant?

Extra Practice
Practice Masters 19–20

Support for
English Language Learners

Instructional feedback is an important part of classroom instruction. However, when working with English Language Learners, it is important to recognize cultural differences pertaining to instructional feedback. Students from some cultures perceive instructional feedback given publicly as embarrassing, while students from other cultures might expect and desire explicit corrective feedback as soon as they make a mistake. Give students feedback individually. Over time, help students understand that feedback is a common and constructive practice in U.S. classrooms.

T38

Before you join one letter to another, look at the way the first letter ends.

Undercurve-to-Downcurve Joining
The undercurve swings wide and forms the top of the downcurve of the next letter.

la   do   to   ice   clay

Overcurve-to-Downcurve Joining
The overcurve crosses at the baseline, then continues up and wide to form the top of the downcurve letter.

ya   go   zo   jam   yawn

Checkstroke-to-Downcurve Joining
The checkstroke ending ⌣ swings right to form the top of the downcurve letter.

oo   bo   wa   bay   wool

Undercurve-to-Overcurve Joining
The undercurve swings wide and forms the top of the overcurve of the next letter.

nn   mm   na   funny   France

Stop and Check
Circle a word you wrote that has good joinings.   39

Objective: To practice writing letter joinings.

1 Model

Model each type of joining on the board as you say the stroke descriptions for the letters you write.

Repeat the stroke descriptions as students use their index finger to trace the letters and joinings on their desktop.

Focus on the checkstroke-to-downcurve joining. Explain that, because the checkstroke letters end at the midline, the initial stroke for the following letter is changed. Demonstrate these joinings on the board, emphasizing the connecting stroke. The use of colored chalk or markers to highlight the joinings might be helpful.

2 Practice

Remind students to position their book and grip their pencil correctly for writing.

Remind students that when they come to this symbol ✓, they should stop writing and circle their best letter.

3 Evaluate

Tell students it is important to make their writing easy for others to read. Remind them to complete the **Stop and Check** activity at the end of the lesson.

✓ **Use** these questions to help students evaluate their cursive writing:

- Which of your joinings are satisfactory?
- Which of your joinings need improvement?

Writing Center

Begin a discussion about cartoons students enjoy. Ask students why they think the cartoons are entertaining. Then ask them to write a paragraph about a favorite cartoon or about something comical they have seen or experienced. Remind students to use their best cursive handwriting.

Review

Checkstroke Alert

Objective: To review lowercase cursive **a, d, g, o, c,** and **q;** to practice writing the checkstroke joinings.

1 Review

Review the stroke descriptions, and model again any letters students might be having difficulty writing. Point out that cursive letters **a, d, g, o, c,** and **q** all begin with a downcurve.

Ask a volunteer to give a verbal description of one of these letters: **a, d, g, o, c, q.** Challenge the other students to identify the letter being described and then write it on guidelines on the board.

See the **Corrective Strategies** in the Appendix for techniques in correcting common problems in your students' handwriting.

Digital Resources for Handwriting

Interactive digital resources for whole-class instruction include proper pencil and paper positions for right- and left-handed students, letter animations that show how to form each letter, and letter activities. (Interactive whiteboard compatible.)

2 Practice

Remind students to position their book and grip their pencil correctly for writing.

Ask students to carefully write the words on student page 40, remembering to form their letters with correct strokes so they will have proper shape. Then have them read and follow the directions for the **Checkstroke Alert** near the bottom of the page.

3 Evaluate

Tell students it is important to make their writing easy for others to read.

Proper Shape, Size, Spacing, and Slant make words easy to read. Ask:

• Did you write with correct strokes so your letters have good shape?

• Did you use the guidelines to write letters with correct size?

• Did you allow good spacing between letters in words?

• Does your writing have uniform forward slant?

Support for
English Language Learners

Use reciprocal teaching to have students teach one another how to write cursive letters. First explain the three cognitive strategies of reciprocal teaching: visualizing, summarizing, questioning. Tell students they will need to picture the letter and recall the steps in its formation. Students can use questioning to help clarify content and to lead their partners to evaluate their own work.

T40

Application

Write the paragraph about Amazon rain forest animals on the guidelines below. Use your best cursive, and remember to indent the first line and leave room for margins.

The Amazon rain forest is home to incredible animals. Toucans are beautiful birds with extremely long bills. Jaguars live on the rain forest floor, climb trees, and swim in water. And the anaconda might be the Amazon's most famous animal. It is the world's heaviest snake!

Stop and Check
Circle your best letter.

41

Application

Objective: To write a paragraph about the rain forest using legible cursive handwriting.

1 Review

Read aloud the text on student page 41, and review the names of the animals often found in a rain forest. Remind students they will write the paragraph using their best cursive handwriting.

Remind students to correctly form **a, d, g, o, c,** and **q** when they write.

2 Practice

Remind students to position their book and grip their pencil correctly for writing.

Ask students to carefully write the paragraph about some well-known rain forest animals. Remind them to form their letters with correctly written strokes.

Point out that the first line of the paragraph is indented, and remind students to leave room for margins.

3 Evaluate

Tell students it is important to make their writing easy for others to read. Remind them to complete the **Stop and Check** activity at the bottom of the lesson.

Use these questions to help students evaluate their cursive writing:

- Are your slant strokes pulled toward the baseline?
- Is there proper space between each letter and word?
- Do your letters look like the models?
- Did you use proper slant?

Tips From an
Occupational Therapist

Planting and gardening are fine-motor activities that can be done inside the classroom or outside near the school. Have students dig a small hole outside with a hand shovel, or if working inside, provide them with small pots. Plant small seeds and have students water the plants with a spray bottle or watering can every other day. If you are able to create a small garden, have students assist with weeding or other maintenance tasks.

T41

Cursive Writing

In the Real World

Objective: To practice writing in cursive legibly in a real-world setting.

Cursive Writing

In the Real World

The more you practice writing in cursive, the easier it will be!

Learning cursive will help you write more quickly. This can be important when taking notes in class.

In class, you wrote a summary of what you learned about the sun. After you finished, you highlighted five words that you had spelled incorrectly. On the guidelines below, write the misspelled words correctly, in cursive. Writing the words again will help you remember them.

The sun is the center of our solar system. It is the closest star to Earth and gives Earth lite and heat. The sun's surface is made up of gas that is always muving. Prominences are clowds of gas that explode from the surface, and solar flares are qwite larger explosions. There are also cool, darc patches called sunspots.

42

---

1 Model

Read aloud the text on student page 42. Review the summary written about the sun and discuss why it is important to spell words correctly.

Model the activity. Write the first sentence in cursive on the board, making an obvious spelling error. Invite volunteers to identify the misspelled word and to spell the word correctly. Write the word correctly on the board.

Review the stroke descriptions and model again any letters students might be having difficulty writing.

2 Practice

Remind students to position their book and grip their pencil correctly for writing.

Ask students to carefully write the misspelled words on the page correctly in cursive.

3 Evaluate

Tell students it is important to make their writing easy for others to read.

✓ **Use** these questions to help students evaluate their writing:

- Did you write with correct strokes so your letters have good shape?
- Did you use the guidelines to write letters with correct size?
- Did you follow the models so your writing would be legible?

Support for
English Language Learners

Remind students that a dictionary will help them spell and pronounce words correctly and understand what words mean. Give each student or pair of students a dictionary. Practice finding a few words together as a class. Direct students to use the guide words at the top of each page to locate the word they are looking for. Review the information included in an entry. Then give students a short list of words to find with a partner, taking turns spelling and pronouncing the words. Have students write a sentence using each word. It might be helpful to have students create their own word banks.

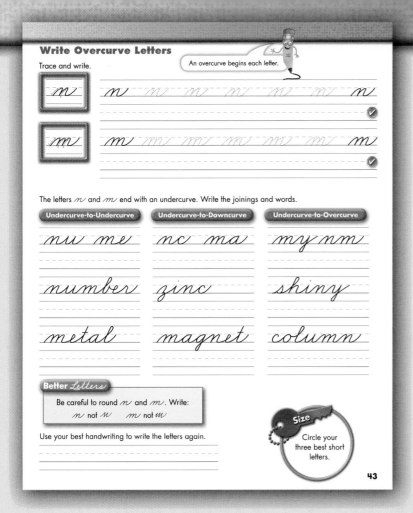

Write Overcurve Letters

Trace and write.

An overcurve begins each letter.

The letters n and m end with an undercurve. Write the joinings and words.

Undercurve-to-Undercurve | **Undercurve-to-Downcurve** | **Undercurve-to-Overcurve**

nu me | nc ma | my nm

number | zinc | shiny

metal | magnet | column

Better Letters

Be careful to round n and m. Write:
n not w m not w

Use your best handwriting to write the letters again.

Size — Circle your three best short letters.

43

Letter Models and Stroke Descriptions

1. Overcurve; slant.
2. Overcurve; slant; undercurve.

1. Overcurve; slant.
2. Overcurve; slant.
3. Overcurve; slant; undercurve.

Objective: To practice and master lowercase cursive **n** and **m**.

1 Model

Talk about the width of lowercase cursive **n** and **m**. Help students compare the letters by asking:

- Which letter is wider, **n** or **m**? *(m)*
- How many times does **m** touch the midline? *(four times)*

Write cursive **n** and **m** on guidelines on the board as you say the stroke descriptions. Ask students to use their index finger to trace **n** and **m** several times in their book. Then model these joinings:

- undercurve-to-undercurve: **me**
- undercurve-to-downcurve: **nc**
- undercurve-to-overcurve: **ny**

Content Connection — Technology

Have students type a book review or journal entry on the computer using a word processing program. Explain to them how to use the spell-check function to check their spelling. Encourage students to write in a word journal any of the words they spelled incorrectly. After students have spell-checked their work, have them reread their writing on the screen to make sure there are no other mistakes in spelling, grammar, or punctuation. Help students save or print their work.

2 Practice

Remind students to position their book and grip their pencil correctly for writing.

Ask students to carefully trace the shaded letters with pencil. Then have them write the letters, joinings, and words on the page.

Remind students that when they come to this symbol, they should stop writing and circle their best letter.

3 Evaluate

Tell students it is important to make their writing easy for others to read. Remind them to complete all **Stop and Check** activities. Use the **Better Letters** box on the student page to help students evaluate their cursive **n** and **m**.

Proper size makes each letter easy to read. Ask:

- Do your tall letters touch the headline?
- Do your short letters stop at the midline?

School/Home Extra Practice
Practice Masters 21–22

T43

Letter Models and Stroke Descriptions

1. Overcurve; slant; undercurve.
2. Slant; loop back; overcurve.

1. Overcurve; slant; undercurve. Lift.
2. Slant.

Objective: To practice and master lowercase cursive **y** and **x**.

Write Overcurve Letters
Trace and write.

An overcurve begins each letter.

The letter y ends with an overcurve. The letter x ends with an undercurve. Write the joinings and words.

Overcurve-to-Undercurve
ye ys
year
days

Overcurve-to-Overcurve
yn ym
lynx
symbol

Undercurve-to-Undercurve
xp xt
expect
next

Better Letters
Be careful to round y and x. Write:
y not y   x not x

Use your best handwriting to write the letters again.

44

Stop and Check
Circle your best y and your best x.

---

1 Model

Talk about cursive **y** and **x**. Ask:
- How many overcurves are in **y**? *(two)*
- Where does the overcurve in **x** end? *(near the midline)*

Write cursive **y** and **x** on guidelines on the board as you say the stroke descriptions. Use skywriting (see Appendix) to model writing **y** and **x** in the air. Then model these joinings:
- overcurve-to-undercurve: **ys**
- overcurve-to-overcurve: **yn**
- undercurve-to-undercurve: **xp**

2 Practice

Remind students to position their book and grip their pencil correctly for writing.

Ask students to begin at the correct position and carefully trace the shaded letters with pencil. Then have them write the letters, joinings, and words on the page.

Remind students that when they come to this symbol ✓, they should stop writing and circle their best letter.

3 Evaluate

Tell students it is important to make their writing easy for others to read. Remind them to complete all **Stop and Check** activities, including the one at the end of the lesson.

✓ **Use** the **Better Letters** box on the student page and these questions to help students evaluate their cursive **y** and **x**:
- Is your **y** about the same width as the model?
- Is your **x** crossed near the middle of the slant stroke?

Extra Practice
Practice Masters 23–24

Support for
English Language Learners

Spend time teaching students the names of days and months. Additionally, teach the words *second, minute, hour, day, week, month, year, decade,* and *leap year.* Teaching time measurement is more effective with hands-on, repetitive activities. Use timers, clocks, and pictures when you talk about seconds, minutes, and hours. Use calendars when you talk about days, weeks, months, and years. Have students write a sentence to illustrate the use of each word.

T44

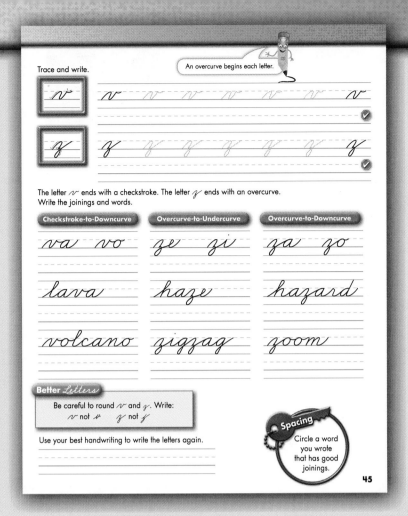

Trace and write.

An overcurve begins each letter.

The letter v ends with a checkstroke. The letter z ends with an overcurve. Write the joinings and words.

Checkstroke-to-Downcurve	Overcurve-to-Undercurve	Overcurve-to-Downcurve
va vo	*ze zi*	*za zo*
lava	*haze*	*hazard*
volcano	*zigzag*	*zoom*

Better *Letters*

Be careful to round v and z. Write:
v not u z not y

Use your best handwriting to write the letters again.

Spacing
Circle a word you wrote that has good joinings.

45

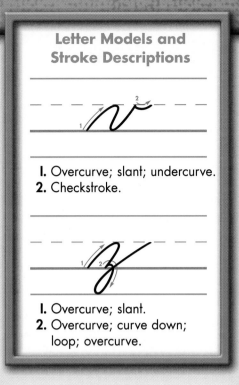

Letter Models and Stroke Descriptions

1. Overcurve; slant; undercurve.
2. Checkstroke.

1. Overcurve; slant.
2. Overcurve; curve down; loop; overcurve.

Objective: To practice and master lowercase cursive **v** and **z**.

---

1 Model

Talk about cursive **v** and **z**. Ask:
- How does **v** end? *(with a checkstroke)*
- Where does the loop close in **z**? *(near the baseline)*

Write cursive **v** and **z** on guidelines on the board as you say the stroke descriptions. Use skywriting to model writing **v** and **z** in the air.

Ask students to use their index finger to trace cursive **v** and **z** several times in their book. Then model these joinings:
- checkstroke-to-downcurve: **va**
- overcurve-to-undercurve: **ze**
- overcurve-to-downcurve: **zo**

2 Practice

Remind students to position their book and grip their pencil correctly for writing.

Ask students to start at the correct position and carefully trace the shaded letters with pencil. Then have them write the letters, joinings, and words on the page.

Remind students that when they come to this symbol ✓, they should stop writing and circle their best letter.

3 Evaluate

Tell students it is important to make their writing easy for others to read. Remind them to complete all **Stop and Check** activities. Use the **Better Letters** box on the student page to help students evaluate their cursive **v** and **z**.

Proper spacing makes each letter easy to read. Ask:
- Does your writing have proper spacing?
- Is there enough space for O between your letters?

School Home **Extra Practice**
Practice Masters 25–26

Writing Center

Invite students to research the topic of volcanoes using the Internet and/or library resources. If you wish, select several informational sites that you have previewed on the topic. Then have students use the research and images they collected to write a one-page report on volcanoes. (Internet use should be carefully monitored).

Review

Checkstroke Alert

Objective: To review lowercase cursive **n, m, y, x, v,** and **z;** to practice writing the checkstroke joining.

Review (student page)

Write the words.

animals

ox   viper   fox

chimpanzee   buzzard

yak   hyena   turkey

zebra   zoo   vulture

Checkstroke Alert Each word has a checkstroke joining at the midline. Write the words.

mouse   ostrich   boar

lion   oxen

My writing has good ___. ☐
My writing has good ___. ☐
My writing has good ___. ☐
My writing has good ___. ☐

46

---

1 Review

Review the stroke descriptions, and model again any letters students might be having difficulty writing. Point out that the letters **n, m, y, x, v,** and **z** begin with an overcurve.

Ask a volunteer to give a verbal description of one of these letters: **n, m, y, x, v, z.** Challenge the other students to identify the letter being described and then write it on guidelines on the board.

See the **Corrective Strategies** in the Appendix for techniques in correcting common problems in your students' handwriting.

▶ Digital Resources for Handwriting

Interactive digital resources for whole-class instruction include proper pencil and paper positions for right- and left-handed students, letter animations that show how to form each letter, and letter activities. (Interactive whiteboard compatible.)

2 Practice

Remind students to position their book and grip their pencil correctly for writing.

Ask students to carefully write the words on the page, remembering to form their letters with correct strokes so they will have proper shape. Then have them read and follow the directions for the **Checkstroke Alert** near the bottom of the page.

3 Evaluate

Tell students it is important to make their writing easy for others to read.

Proper Shape, Size, Spacing, and Slant make words easy to read. Ask:

- Did you write with correct strokes so your letters have good shape?
- Did you use the guidelines to write letters with correct size?
- Did you allow good spacing between letters and words?
- Does your writing have uniform forward slant?

Support for English Language Learners

With students, brainstorm a list of animals. Write the animals they suggest on the board. Have students say the name of each animal in their native language. Then have students choose an animal and find pictures of it in books or on the internet. Instruct them to draw a picture of the animal they chose and label it with its name.

Look at the photo below, and read the lists of nouns and adjectives. Circle the three nouns and the three adjectives that you think fit the photo.

Nouns	Adjectives
chimpanzees	asleep
gorillas	excited
hands	five
jungle	hairy
zebras	alert
zoo	two

Write a short paragraph in cursive describing the photo. Use the six words you circled. Remember to indent the first line of your paragraph and leave space for margins.

Stop and Check
Circle your best letter.

47

Application

Objective: To write adjectives describing animals using legible handwriting.

1 Review

Read aloud the text and the writing prompt on student page 47. Remind students that nouns are naming words and adjectives are words that describe nouns. Call on students to read the nouns and adjectives on the page.

Remind students to correctly form **n, m, y, x, v, z** when they write their paragraph.

2 Practice

Remind students to position their book and grip their pencil correctly for writing.

Ask students to carefully write a paragraph describing the photo on the student page using the nouns and adjectives they selected. Remind them to form their letters with correctly written strokes so they will have good shape.

Remind students to indent the first line of their paragraph and leave space for margins.

3 Evaluate

Tell students it is important to make their writing easy for others to read. Remind them to complete the **Stop and Check** activity at the end of the lesson.

✓ **Use** these questions to help students evaluate their cursive writing:
- Are your slant strokes pulled toward the baseline?
- Is there proper space between each letter and word?
- Do your letters look like the models?
- Did you use proper slant?

Tips From an
Occupational Therapist

Have students use index cards to create coupon books for a parent or caregiver. On each card, students write a chore that would help out at home (e.g. wash dishes, fold laundry). Have students decorate the cards with markers, punch a hole in the top left corner of each card, and string a ribbon through the holes to make a book. Using a hole puncher strengthens the arches of the hands and encourages an open webspace between the thumb and index finger, which is needed during long writing tasks.

Keys to Legibility

Shape 🔑
describes the strokes that form each letter and give it a unique appearance.

Size 🔑
describes the height of letters.

Spacing 🔑
describes the space between letters, words, and sentences.

Slant 🔑
describes the angle of writing on the paper.

Objective: To practice the four Keys to Legibility.

Keys to Legibility

Write the steps for washing a dog.
Make your writing easy to read.

1. get dog wet

2. wash with shampoo

3. rinse with water

4. brush and dry

48

Handwriting Coach

Keys to Legibility

Review the four Keys to Legibility: Shape, Size, Spacing, and Slant. Write several words on the board with errors in shape, size, spacing, and slant. Ask student volunteers to explain the errors and then rewrite the words correctly with colored chalk or markers.

1 Review

Remind students that good handwriting is legible handwriting. The most important thing to remember is that readers must be able to read a message to understand its meaning.

Brainstorm with students qualities of legible handwriting. Write their responses on the board. These might include neatness, carefully written letters, and letters that are not too crowded.

2 Practice

Remind students to position their book and grip their pencil correctly for writing. Ask students to carefully write the phrases on student page 48.

Emphasize that all four Keys to Legibility work together. Students' writing will be easy to read when they use proper shape, size, spacing, and slant.

Read and discuss with students the activity on student page 49. Then help them as needed to complete the writing activity.

Support for
English Language Learners

To help students understand nouns, remind them that a noun is the name of a **person, place, thing,** or **idea**. Make a chart on the board with these headings. Write an example under each heading (examples: **nurse, playground, swing, swimming**). Ask students to name other nouns and say where they belong on the chart. Write their ideas on the board. Then ask students to choose five nouns and use each noun in a written sentence. Encourage students to read their sentences aloud.

T48

Write the steps for a task you know how to do.

Is your writing easy to read?

Shape
Circle your best letter that has an undercurve beginning.

Size
Circle your best short letter.

Spacing
Circle two words that have space for \ between them.

Slant
Circle a word you wrote that has good slant.

49

3 Evaluate

Tell students it is important to make their writing easy for others to read.

Shape

- Does each letter have its own clear shape?
- Did you end each short undercurve stroke near the midline?
- Did you end each tall undercurve stroke near the headline?

Size

- Did you use the guidelines to write letters with correct size?
- Do your tall letters touch the headline and the baseline?
- Are short letters the same height?

Spacing

- Are your letters neither too close together nor too far apart?
- Is there space for \ between your words?
- Is there space for O between letters in your words?

Slant

- Does your writing have uniform forward slant?
- Did you pull your downstrokes in the proper direction?
- Is your writing easy to read?

Content Connection — Language Arts

Ask students to recall books they have read in which a pet is an important character. Have students say what animal the pet was, who it belonged to, and why it was important in the story. Instruct students to write a short paragraph about the story, including the title of the book, the author, and the name of the pet.

T49

Lowercase Review

Objective: To review lowercase cursive letters.

Lowercase Review

Write undercurve letters.

i   t   u   w   e   l   b

h   f   k   r   s   j   p

Write downcurve letters.

a   d   g   o   c   q

Write overcurve letters.

n   m   y   x   v   z

Circle your best letter in each group above. Write the letters you want to improve.

Write the joinings.

it   ea   ry   ye   ga   wr   bo

50

1 Review

Review the stroke descriptions and model again any letters students might be having difficulty writing.

Ask a volunteer to give a verbal description of one of the letters. Challenge other students to identify the letter being described and then write it on guidelines on the board.

See the **Corrective Strategies** in the Appendix for techniques in correcting common problems in your students' handwriting.

2 Practice

Remind students to position their book and grip their pencil correctly for writing.

Ask students to carefully write the letters on the page, remembering to incorporate correct shape and size and to write with good spacing and uniform slant.

Have students read and follow the directions for the evaluation section. Then have them write the joinings.

3 Evaluate

Tell students it is important to make their writing easy for others to read.

✔ **Use** these questions to help students evaluate their cursive writing:

- Did you write with correct strokes so your letters have good shape?
- Did you use the guidelines to write letters with correct size?
- Did you allow good spacing between your letters?
- Does your writing have uniform forward slant?

Support for
English Language Learners

Create a balance between rote activities and those that develop higher-order thinking skills. Use rote learning to develop letter and word recognition, teach spelling rules, improve aural discrimination, and help students achieve handwriting fluency. To help students develop higher-order thinking skills, create a classroom environment in which students are encouraged to share their thoughts, ask questions, and have many opportunities to write essays, stories, and poems.

Manuscript Maintenance

Manuscript Maintenance
Bicycle Parts

seat — grip — handlebars
rear reflector — crossbar — front reflector
seat post — brake line — tire
reflector — rim
gears — spoke
spoke — chain — pedal — wheel — reflector

Unscramble the name of each bicycle part. Write the names in manuscript.

badlehanrs		atse	
irpg		atse sopt	
ehewl		ossrcarb	
riet		deapl	
mir		toreclfer	
skope		ihcna	

51

Objective: To review and practice manuscript letters.

1 Model

Have students look at the picture and the words on student page 51. Ask students to describe what they remember about the shape, size, spacing, and slant of letters and words written in manuscript.

Review the stroke descriptions and model again any letters students might be having difficulty writing. Refer students to the manuscript alphabet on student page 10 for more guidance.

Ask a volunteer to give a verbal description of one of the letters. Challenge other students to identify the letter being described and then write it on guidelines on the board.

2 Practice

Remind students to position their book and grip their pencil correctly for writing.

Ask students to read the directions and unscramble the names of the bicycle parts on student page 51. Tell them to write the names of the parts in manuscript, remembering to form the letters carefully so they are legible.

3 Evaluate

Tell students it is important to make their writing easy for others to read.

✓ **Use** these questions to help students evaluate their writing:
- Did you write with correct strokes so your letters have correct shape?
- Did you write letters with good size to fit the writing space?
- Did you allow good spacing?
- Did you maintain uniform vertical slant?

Writing Center

Have students write a personal narrative about a bike trip they took through their neighborhood. Ask them to include details about who they were with, what they saw, and where they biked. Invite students to read their narrative to a partner.

Numeral Models and Stroke Descriptions

I. Slant.

I. Slant.
2. Curve forward; slant.
3. Curve right.

I. Slant.
2. Curve forward and back.
3. Curve forward and back.

I. Slant.
2. Slide right. Lift.
3. Slant.

I. Slant.
2. Curve forward and back. Lift.
3. Slide right.

Objective: To practice and master writing cursive numerals.

T52

Cursive Numerals

Write the missing numerals.

14, 16, 18, _____, _____, 24, _____

Write the missing numerals.

78, 79, _____, _____, 82, 83, _____

Write the odd numbers between 1 and 13.

1, _____ _____ _____ _____ _____ 13

Write the even numbers between 10 and 20.

10, _____ _____ _____ _____ , 20

Here are two magic squares. The sum of the numbers in a magic square's rows and columns is always the same. Fill in the missing numerals.

52

---

1 Model

Write cursive **1** on guidelines on the board as you say the stroke description. Use skywriting to model writing **1** in the air. Have students stand and say the stroke description with you as they write cursive **1** in the air.

Have a volunteer write cursive numerals **1–5** on the board, naming the strokes and demonstrating good shape, size, and slant. Have another volunteer do the same with the numerals **6–10**.

2 Practice

Remind students to position their book and grip their pencil correctly for writing.

Ask students why they think writing legible numerals is important. Have them write their school's address and telephone number on paper. Then have them exchange papers so a classmate can evaluate the numerals for legibility.

Ask students to read and follow the directions on student pages 52 and 53, writing the numbers on the pages using their best cursive handwriting.

Support for English Language Learners

Say the names of the numerals and have students repeat them in chorus. Listen for the correct pronunciation of each numeral. Have students write each numeral on a sheet of paper or slate and its English name next to it. Organize students into groups, and encourage groups to say aloud the numbers from the magic squares on the student page.

Write these facts about time in your best cursive handwriting.

A minute is 60 seconds.

An hour is 60 minutes.

A day is 24 hours.

A week is 7 days.

A year is 12 months.

A year is 365 days.

A leap year is 366 days.

A decade is 10 years.

53

3 Evaluate

Tell students it is important to make their writing easy for others to read.

✓ **Use** these questions to help students evaluate their cursive numerals:

- Does your **1** begin at the headline?
- Does your **2** begin with a short slant stroke?
- Are the top and bottom of your **3** about the same size?
- Is the slide right of your **4** on the midline?
- Does your **5** touch both the headline and the baseline?
- Does the loop of your **6** end at the baseline?
- Does the top of your **7** have a slight doublecurve?
- Does your **8** begin just below the headline?
- Is your **9** written with correct slant?
- Is there correct space between the **1** and the **0** in your **10**?

Numeral Models and Stroke Descriptions

6
1. Curve down and forward; loop.

7
1. Slant.
2. Doublecurve.
3. Slant.

8
1. Curve back and down; curve back; slant up.

9
1. Downcurve; undercurve.
2. Slant.

10
1. Slant. Lift.
2. Downcurve; undercurve.

Extra Practice
Practice Masters 27–28

Tips From an
Occupational Therapist

Help students learn geometric shapes while practicing handwriting. Introduce geometric shapes such as circles, squares, rectangles, cones, cylinders, cubes, pyramids, spheres, octagons, hexagons, and triangles. Provide students with geometric blocks or shapes for them to use as patterns. Ask them to use the blocks to draw outlines of the shapes on construction paper and then cut out the shapes with scissors. Then have students write a label on each shape to identify the name of the shape and the number of sides it has. Cutting complex angles and curves improves fine-motor manipulation skills.

T53

Background Information

Langston Hughes (1902–1967) grew up listening to jazz and blues music. He expressed his passion for jazz and blues by using music themes, images, and rhythms in his poetry. Much of Hughes's poetry focuses on his experiences living in the Harlem neighborhood in New York City. Harlem was a popular neighborhood among artists, writers, and musicians in Hughes's lifetime.

Objective: To read a poem and discuss its meaning.

April Rain Song

Let the rain kiss you.
Let the rain beat upon your head with silver liquid drops.
Let the rain sing you a lullaby.

The rain makes still pools on the sidewalk.
The rain makes running pools in the gutter.
The rain plays a little sleep-song on our roof at night—

And I love the rain.

Langston Hughes

54

55

Questions for Discussion

1. Why do you think the poet included the month in the title?

2. Do you agree that raindrops are silver-colored? Explain.

3. Line 3 describes the sound of the rain as a lullaby. Which line makes a similar comparison?

4. Which two lines describe how the rain behaves on the ground?

5. Which three verbs in the poem describe the rain as though it is a person?

Writing Extension

Ask students to write their own poems about rain or snow. Have volunteers share their poems with the class.

Instructional Manipulatives

Manipulatives in your classroom handwriting center or work station can reinforce and extend your handwriting instruction, especially for kinesthetic learners. Along with a model of the alphabet and a variety of types of paper and writing implements, you might include the following manipulatives to help students practice proper letter and numeral formation.

- Touch and Trace Cards™ Manuscript and Cursive
- Wikki Stix®
- Magnetic Letters
- Write-on, Write-off Magnetic Dry Erase Board

Be sure to model how to use each manipulative before placing it in the handwriting work station. For example, model how to use a Touch and Trace Card with Wikki Stix to form the letter A. See page Z14 for additional work station suggestions.

Writing Uppercase Letters

Objective: To write uppercase cursive letters.

1 Model

Write the basic strokes on guidelines on the board as you name each stroke. Invite students to say the stroke names as they write the strokes in the air. Point out that uppercase cursive letters are formed from these basic strokes. Invite volunteers to identify the basic strokes in several of the uppercase letters on student page 56.

Model writing several letters, including a letter with a descender, noting the placement of each letter on the guidelines. Remind students that all uppercase letters are tall.

2 Practice

Remind students to position their book and grip their pencil correctly for writing.

Ask students to carefully write the letters on the page.

Have students complete the evaluation activity at the bottom of the page.

3 Evaluate

Tell students it is important to make their writing easy for others to read.

✓ **Use** these questions to help students evaluate their lowercase cursive letters:

- Did you use good strokes so your letters have correct shape?
- Do your letters rest on the baseline?
- Do your letters have uniform forward slant?

Support for
English Language Learners

Review with students the sound each letter makes. Say the sound and have students repeat it after you. Correct any mispronunciations students make. Write each letter on the board. Have students think of a few words that begin with each letter. Record students' suggestions next to each letter. Then have students copy the letters and words from the board onto paper. Encourage groups or teams of students to listen and speak to one another as they practice the words.

Beginning Strokes

The uppercase letters are grouped by their strokes.

Downcurve Letters
Trace downcurve strokes and letters.

Curve Forward Letters
Trace curve forward-slant strokes and curve forward letters.

Overcurve and Doublecurve Letters
Trace overcurve strokes and letters.

Trace doublecurve strokes and letters.

Undercurve-Loop and Undercurve-Slant Letters
Trace undercurve-loop strokes and letters.

Trace undercurve-slant strokes and letters.

57

Beginning Strokes

Objective: To practice writing cursive beginning strokes; to practice writing uppercase cursive letters.

1 Model

Point out the shaded uppercase letters on student page 57, and explain that each begins with or includes a specific stroke: downcurve, curve forward, overcurve, doublecurve, undercurve-loop, or undercurve-slant.

Review the description for each stroke (see pages T14–T15).

Model examples of the strokes using skywriting, and have students write them in the air with you as they say the stroke description for each one.

2 Practice

Remind students to position their book and grip their pencil correctly for writing.

Ask students to trace the beginning strokes and then the letters in each section on student page 57.

Encourage students to summarize what they notice about the strokes and letters on the page in relation to the Keys to Legibility.

3 Evaluate

Tell students it is important to make their writing easy for others to read.

Use these questions to help students evaluate their writing:
- Did you use good strokes so your letters have correct shape?
- Do your letters rest on the baseline?
- Do your letters have uniform forward slant?

Content Connection Fine Arts

Show students examples of abstract paintings. Provide students with paint, paintbrushes, and large sheets of paper. Have them choose two beginning strokes to incorporate into their own abstract work of art. Display the artwork around the room, and invite students to find the beginning strokes in each piece.

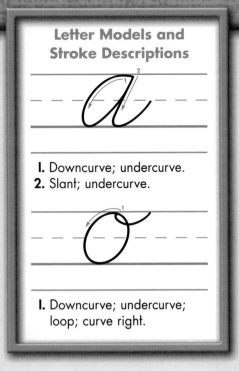

Letter Models and Stroke Descriptions

1. Downcurve; undercurve.
2. Slant; undercurve.

1. Downcurve; undercurve; loop; curve right.

Objective: To practice and master uppercase cursive **A** and **O**.

Write Downcurve Letters

Trace and write.

A downcurve begins each letter.

Joining Alert a is joined to the letter that follows, but O is not.

Write the words and sentences.

Alabama   Oklahoma

America is beautiful.

Our flag flies proudly.

Better Letters
Make sure to close a and O. Write:
a not a O not O

Use your best handwriting to write the letters again.

58

Stop and Check
Circle your best joining.

1 Model

Talk about cursive **A** and **O**. Ask:
- How many strokes are in **A**? *(four)*
- How many pauses are in **O**? *(none)*

Write cursive **A** and **O** on guidelines on the board.

Remind students that **O** is not joined to the letter that follows. Point out the undercurve ending of **A**. Then model these joinings:
- undercurve-to-undercurve: **Al**
- undercurve-to-downcurve: **Ad**
- undercurve-to-overcurve: **Am**

2 Practice

Remind students to position their book and grip their pencil correctly for writing.

Ask students to carefully trace the shaded letters with pencil. Then have them write the letters, words, and sentences on the page.

Remind students that when they come to this symbol ✓, they should stop writing and circle their best letter.

3 Evaluate

Tell students it is important to make their writing easy for others to read. Remind them to complete all **Stop and Check** activities.

✓ **Use** the **Better Letters** box on the student page and these questions to help students evaluate their cursive **A** and **O**:
- Does your **A** slant forward?
- Does your **O** begin below the headline?

School Home Extra Practice
Practice Masters 29–30

Support for
English Language Learners

Be aware that capitalization rules vary by language. Teach English capitalization rules to help students determine when and how to use capital letters.

Model capitalization rules with examples on the board. Using the names of students in your class, write sentences to model correct and incorrect capitalization. For example, write **My name is Giselle Lozano. I live in Texas.** and **My name is giselle lozano. I live in texas.** Have students write their own sentences.

T58

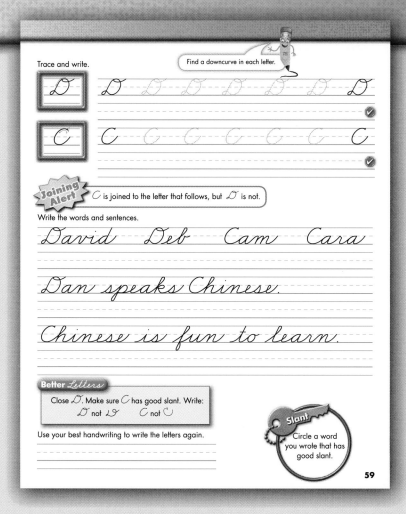

Trace and write.

Find a downcurve in each letter.

$\mathcal{D}$ $\mathcal{D}$ $\mathcal{D}$ $\mathcal{D}$ $\mathcal{D}$ $\mathcal{D}$ $\mathcal{D}$

$\mathcal{C}$ $\mathcal{C}$ $\mathcal{C}$ $\mathcal{C}$ $\mathcal{C}$ $\mathcal{C}$ $\mathcal{C}$

Joining Alert $\mathcal{C}$ is joined to the letter that follows, but $\mathcal{D}$ is not.

Write the words and sentences.

David Deb Cam Cara

Dan speaks Chinese.

Chinese is fun to learn.

Better Letters
Close $\mathcal{D}$. Make sure $\mathcal{C}$ has good slant. Write:
$\mathcal{D}$ not $\mathcal{LD}$ $\mathcal{C}$ not $\mathcal{U}$

Use your best handwriting to write the letters again.

Slant Circle a word you wrote that has good slant.

59

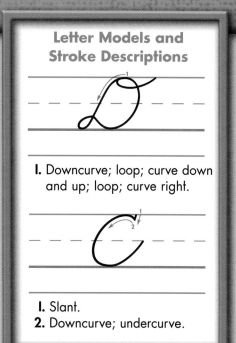

Letter Models and Stroke Descriptions

I. Downcurve; loop; curve down and up; loop; curve right.

I. Slant.
2. Downcurve; undercurve.

Objective: To practice and master uppercase cursive **D** and **C**.

1 Model

Talk about cursive **D** and **C**. Ask:
- How many loops are in **D**? *(two)*
- How does **C** begin? *(with a slant stroke)*

Use skywriting (see Appendix) to model writing cursive **D** and **C** in the air.

Remind students that **D** is not joined to the letter that follows. Point out the undercurve ending of **C**. Then model these joinings:
- undercurve-to-undercurve: **Ci**
- undercurve-to-downcurve: **Ca**
- undercurve-to-overcurve: **Cy**

2 Practice

Remind students to position their book and grip their pencil correctly for writing.

Ask students to carefully trace the shaded letters with pencil. Then have them write the letters, words, and sentences on the page.

Remind students that when they come to this symbol (✓), they should stop writing and circle their best letter.

3 Evaluate

Tell students it is important to make their writing easy for others to read. Remind them to complete all **Stop and Check** activities. Use the **Better Letters** box on the student page to help students evaluate their cursive **D** and **C**.

Proper slant makes each letter easy to read. Ask:
- Do your cursive letters have uniform forward slant?
- Did you pull the downstrokes in the proper direction?

School Home Extra Practice
Practice Masters 31–32

Writing Center

Put the **A, O, D,** and **C** *Touch and Trace Cards* in the Writing Center so students can check their knowledge of letter formation. For each card, students should follow these steps:

I. Look at the card. Identify the letter and look at the arrow that shows where to begin.
2. Trace the letter with eyes closed. Follow the correct stroke sequence.
3. Check the stroke formation with eyes open.
4. Write the letter on paper, making sure to use correct stroke sequence.

T59

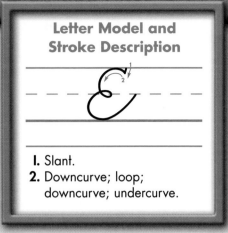

Letter Model and Stroke Description

1. Slant.
2. Downcurve; loop; downcurve; undercurve.

Objective: To practice and master uppercase cursive **E**.

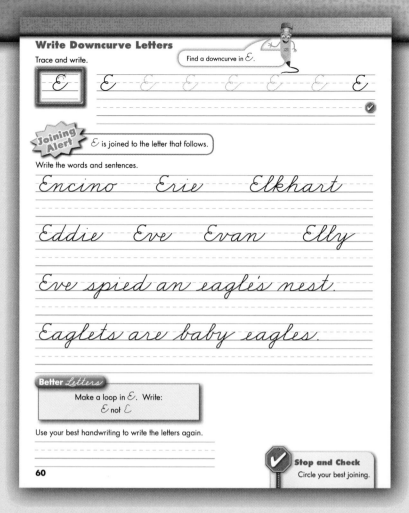

Write Downcurve Letters

Trace and write.

Find a downcurve in $\mathcal{E}$.

Joining Alert $\mathcal{E}$ is joined to the letter that follows.

Write the words and sentences.

Encino   Erie   Elkhart

Eddie   Eve   Evan   Elly

Eve spied an eagle's nest.

Eaglets are baby eagles.

Better *Letters*
Make a loop in $\mathcal{E}$. Write:
$\mathcal{E}$ not $\mathcal{C}$

Use your best handwriting to write the letters again.

60

Stop and Check
Circle your best joining.

1 Model

Talk about cursive **E**. Ask:
- How many loops are in **E**? *(one)*
- How does **E** begin? *(with a slant stroke)*

Write cursive **E** on guidelines as you say the stroke description.

Point out the undercurve ending of **E**. Model these joinings:
- undercurve-to-undercurve: **El**
- undercurve-to-downcurve: **Ed**
- undercurve-to-overcurve: **Ev**

2 Practice

Remind students to position their book and grip their pencil correctly for writing.

Ask students to carefully trace the shaded letters with pencil. Then have them write the letters, words, and sentences on the page.

Remind students that when they come to this symbol, they should stop writing and circle their best letter.

3 Evaluate

Tell students it is important to make their writing easy for others to read. Remind them to complete all **Stop and Check** activities, including the one at the end of the lesson.

Use the **Better Letters** box on the student page to help students evaluate their cursive **E**. Ask:
- Does your **E** have good slant? Is your loop near the midline?

Extra Practice
Practice Master 33

Support for
English Language Learners

Distribute blank bingo cards. Write a list of animals on the board. Have students fill in their bingo grids—except for the free space in the center—with the listed words in a random order. Call out each word. When students find a called word on their card, have them cover it with a counter. When a student believes he or she has a winning sequence, ask the student to read back the words covered on his or her card. This game also provides an opportunity to review the terms *horizontal*, *vertical*, and *diagonal*.

T60

Joining $\mathcal{A}$, $\mathcal{C}$, and $\mathcal{E}$

$\mathcal{A}$, $\mathcal{C}$, and $\mathcal{E}$ are joined to the letter that follows. The undercurve swings up to the midline to form the first curve of the next letter. The joining must be wide enough to allow room for joining to the next letter.

Write the words and sentence.

Adam   Abby   Ajay   Ann

Cory   Chloe   Cam   Clay

Eva   Eric   Emma   Ethan

Eve spied an eagle's nest.

The cursive letters $\mathcal{A}$, $\mathcal{C}$, and $\mathcal{E}$ are joined to the letter that follows.

Stop and Check
Circle your best joining. **61**

Objective: To practice writing **A, C,** and **E** joinings.

1 Model

Tell students that **A, C,** and **E** are joined to the letter that follows. Model on the board how the undercurve swings up to the midline to form the first curve of the next letter.

Remind students that they should make sure their joinings are wide enough to allow room for the next letter.

Emphasize correct joining strokes by writing any word on the board and then using colored chalk or marker to highlight the joining strokes. Help students realize that incorrect joining strokes will make their writing less legible.

2 Practice

Remind students to position their book and grip their pencil correctly for writing.

Ask students to carefully write the words and sentence on the page.

3 Evaluate

Tell students it is important to make their writing easy for others to read.Remind them to complete the **Stop and Check** activity at the end of the lesson.

✓ **Use** these questions to help students evaluate their cursive writing:

- Which of your joinings are satisfactory?
- Which of your joinings need improvement?
- Are your **A, C,** and **E** joinings wide enough?

Tips From an
Occupational Therapist

Gather several different sizes of plastic and glass bottles with small necks, a few turkey basters, metal spoons, and small buckets of water. Instruct students to use the turkey basters to transfer water from the buckets into the bottles. By squeezing the bulbs of the turkey basters, students will improve fine-motor strength, endurance, and precision. Then have students use the metal spoon to gently tap the bottle necks to produce a sound. Challenge students to see if they can play a song on the bottles.

Objective: To review uppercase cursive **A, O, D, C,** and **E**.

---

1 Review

Review the stroke descriptions, and model again any letters students might be having difficulty writing. Point out that **A, O, D, C,** and **E** begin with a downcurve or a short slant followed by a downcurve.

Ask a volunteer to give a verbal description of one of the letters. Challenge other students to identify the letter being described and then write it on guidelines on the board.

See the **Corrective Strategies** in the Appendix for techniques in correcting common problems in your students' handwriting.

2 Practice

Remind students to position their book and grip their pencil correctly for writing.

Ask students to carefully write the words and paragraph on the page, remembering to form their letters with correct strokes so they will have proper shape.

3 Evaluate

Tell students it is important to make their writing easy for others to read.

Proper Shape, Size, Spacing, and Slant make words easy to read. Ask:

- Did you write with correct strokes so your letters have good shape?
- Are your short letters half the height of your tall letters?
- Is there proper space between each letter and word?
- Did you use proper slant?

Digital Resources for Handwriting

Interactive digital resources for whole-class instruction include proper pencil and paper positions for right- and left-handed students, letter animations that show how to form each letter, and letter activities. (Interactive whiteboard compatible.)

Support for English Language Learners

Students might struggle with the multiple-meaning word *desert*. Explain to students that the meaning of the noun form of *desert* is a dry, hot landform and that the verb form of *desert* means to leave a place or people behind. Help students with the different pronunciations of the two words. Also point out that the similarly spelled *dessert* has a completely different meaning: a sweet food eaten at the end of a meal. Have students write a sentence using each word appropriately.

T62

Application

Road Trip

Plan a road trip across the country, starting in an eastern state along the Atlantic Ocean and finishing in a western state along the Pacific Ocean. Choose five cities you will visit, including your starting and ending city.

Here's your challenge: Choose cities that begin with each of these uppercase letters: a, C, D, E, and O.

Write a short paragraph on the guidelines below. Tell which city you will start in, which city you'll end in, and which three cities you'll visit in between. Remember to leave space for margins.

My Road Trip Plan

Stop and Check
Circle your best letter.

63

Objective: To write a road-trip plan using legible cursive handwriting.

1 Review

Review with students how to write **A, O, D, C,** and **E** on the board. Say stroke descriptions aloud and have students trace the letters with their finger on their desk. Practice any joinings that students are having difficulty writing.

Read aloud the directions on student page 63 and the labeled cities and states. Point out the Atlantic and Pacific Oceans on the map, and answer any questions students might have about what they are to do.

2 Practice

Remind students to position their book and grip their pencil correctly for writing.

Ask students to carefully write their road-trip plan, remembering to form their letters with correctly written strokes so they will have good shape.

3 Evaluate

Tell students it is important to make their writing easy for others to read. Remind them to complete the **Stop and Check** activity at the end of the lesson.

Use these questions to help students evaluate their cursive writing:

- Are your slant strokes pulled toward the baseline?
- Do your letters look like the models?
- Is your **A** closed?
- Does your **O** end near the headline?
- Is the loop in your **E** at the midline?

Content Connection — Social Studies

Ask students to choose one of the cities they included on student page 63. Help them use an Internet search engine or other resource to research the city and answer questions such as *What is the population of the city? What attractions could you visit there? What is the average temperature during each season?* Then have students find and print a few pictures of the city. Ask students to present what they learned about their city to the class. (Internet use should be carefully monitored).

Cursive Writing

In the Real World

Objective: To practice writing a personal schedule legibly in cursive.

Cursive Writing

In the Real World

The more you practice writing in cursive, the easier it will be!

Learning cursive will help you write more quickly.
This can be important when writing a personal schedule.

Saturday, October 22nd
10:00 am Art project with Dan
12:30 pm Lunch with Olivia
2:45 pm Soccer game at Eastern Athletic Center
7:15 pm Dinner at Ed's Diner with Cassie

Write the schedule.

64

---

1 Model

Tell students that as they practice writing in cursive, it will become easier and they will write more quickly.

Review the stroke descriptions for any letters that might be difficult for students, and write the letters on the board. The ability to write letters and words automatically will allow them to spend more time thinking about the content of their writing.

2 Practice

Remind students to position their book and grip their pencil correctly for writing.

Ask students to carefully write the schedule on the page.

3 Evaluate

Tell students it is important to make their writing easy for others to read.

☑ **Use** these questions to help students evaluate their cursive writing:

- Did you write with correct strokes so your letters have good shape?
- Did you leave appropriate space between your letters and words?
- Is your writing easy to read?

Support for
English Language Learners

To help students better manage their time, ask them to write their own daily schedules. Remind them to include all the classes and activities they participate in while at school and also those after school, including homework and dinner. Have students self-evaluate their writing. If students are having difficulty turning in homework, help them review their schedules to find a time when they might complete it.

T64

Write Curve Forward Letters

Trace and write.

Both n and m begin with a curve forward stroke.

Joining Alert n and m are joined to the letter that follows.

Write the words and sentences.

Nevada Maryland Maine

Nell went to Montana.

Mountain hikes were fun.

Better Letters

Start m and n just under the headline. Write:
m not m n not n

Use your best handwriting to write the letters again.

Shape Circle your three best letters with an undercurve ending.

65

Letter Models and Stroke Descriptions

1. Curve forward; slant.
2. Overcurve; slant; undercurve.

1. Curve forward; slant.
2. Overcurve; slant.
3. Overcurve; slant; undercurve.

Objective: To practice and master uppercase cursive **N** and **M**.

---

1 Model

Talk about cursive **N** and **M**. Ask:
- How does **N** begin? *(with a curve forward and a slant)*
- Where does **M** end? *(at the midline)*

Write cursive **N** and **M** on guidelines on the board as you say the stroke descriptions. Use skywriting (see Appendix) to model writing **N** and **M** in the air. Then model these joinings:
- undercurve-to-undercurve: **Ne**
- undercurve-to-downcurve: **Ma**
- undercurve-to-overcurve: **My**

2 Practice

Remind students to position their book and grip their pencil correctly for writing.

Ask students to carefully trace the shaded letters with pencil. Then have them write the letters, words, and sentences on the page.

Remind students that when they come to this symbol, they should stop writing and circle their best letter.

3 Evaluate

Tell students it is important to make their writing easy for others to read. Remind them to complete all **Stop and Check** activities. Use the **Better Letters** box on the student page to help students evaluate their cursive **N** and **M**.

Proper shape makes each letter easy to read. Ask:
- Is your **N** about the same width as the model?
- Are the overcurves in your **M** rounded?

School Home Extra Practice
Practice Masters 34–35

Writing Center

Begin a discussion with students about the different states they have visited. Ask students to describe any landforms, such as mountains, valleys, plateaus, plains, or hills that they saw. Have students draw a picture of one of the landforms they saw and write a few sentences to describe it.

T65

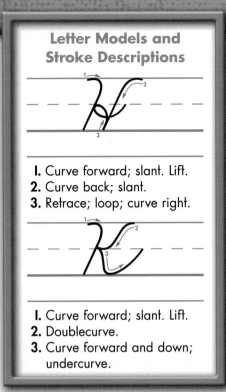

Letter Models and Stroke Descriptions

1. Curve forward; slant. Lift.
2. Curve back; slant.
3. Retrace; loop; curve right.

1. Curve forward; slant. Lift.
2. Doublecurve.
3. Curve forward and down; undercurve.

Objective: To practice and master uppercase cursive **H** and **K**.

Write Curve Forward Letters
Trace and write.

Find a curve forward stroke in each letter.

Joining Alert $\mathcal{H}$ and $\mathcal{K}$ are joined to the letter that follows.

Write the words and sentences.

Hawaii   Kahului   Kauai

Kate likes Honolulu.

Her dad saw orchids there.

Better Letters
Lift after the first stroke for $\mathcal{H}$ and $\mathcal{K}$. Write:
$\mathcal{H}$ not $\mathcal{H}$ $\mathcal{K}$ not $\mathcal{K}$

Use your best handwriting to write the letters again.

Stop and Check
Circle your best $\mathcal{H}$ and your best $\mathcal{K}$.

66

---

1 Model

Talk about cursive **H** and **K**. Ask:
- How many lifts are in **H**? *(one)*
- Where is the lift in **K**? *(after the slant)*

Write cursive **H** and **K** on guidelines on the board as you say the stroke descriptions aloud.

Ask students to use their index finger to trace cursive **H** and **K** several times in their book. Then model these joinings:
- undercurve-to-undercurve: **Kl**
- undercurve-to-downcurve: **Ko**
- curve right-to-overcurve: **Hy**

2 Practice

Remind students to position their book and grip their pencil correctly for writing.

Ask students to carefully trace the shaded letters with pencil. Then have them write the letters, words, and sentences on the page.

Remind students that when they come to this symbol, they should stop writing and circle their best letter.

3 Evaluate

Tell students it is important to make their writing easy for others to read. Remind them to complete all **Stop and Check** activities, including the one at the end of the lesson.

✓ **Use** the **Better Letters** box on the student page and these questions to help students evaluate their cursive **H** and **K**:
- Is your **H** about the same width as the model?
- Does your **K** end at the midline?

School Home **Extra Practice**
Practice Masters 36–37

Support for
English Language Learners

Students might recognize the descriptors *tall* and *short*, but they might not remember that these words can describe letters. To review these descriptors, place pictures illustrating *tall* and *short* on the board. Point to the *tall* picture and say "tall." Point to the *short* picture and say "short." Point out other examples around the room, and invite volunteers to do the same. Have students give examples of tall and short letters.

T66

Trace and write.

Find a curve forward stroke in each letter.

$\mathcal{U}$ $\mathcal{U}$ $\mathcal{U}$ $\mathcal{U}$ $\mathcal{U}$ $\mathcal{U}$ $\mathcal{U}$ $\mathcal{U}$

$\mathcal{Y}$ $\mathcal{Y}$ $\mathcal{Y}$ $\mathcal{Y}$ $\mathcal{Y}$ $\mathcal{Y}$ $\mathcal{Y}$ $\mathcal{Y}$

Joining Alert $\mathcal{U}$ and $\mathcal{Y}$ are joined to the letter that follows.

Write the words and sentences.

Utah   New York   Yuma

The United States is vast.

You and I live there.

Better Letters

Start $\mathcal{U}$ and $\mathcal{Y}$ with a curve forward stroke. Write:
$\mathcal{U}$ not u $\mathcal{Y}$ not y

Use your best handwriting to write the letters again.

Size Circle your three best letters that have a descender.

67

Letter Models and Stroke Descriptions

1. Curve forward; slant; undercurve.
2. Slant; undercurve.

1. Curve forward; slant; undercurve.
2. Slant; loop back; overcurve.

Objective: To practice and master uppercase cursive **U** and **Y**.

---

1 Model

Talk about cursive **U** and **Y**. Ask:
- How many undercurves are in **U**? *(two)*
- How does **Y** end? *(with an overcurve)*

Write cursive **U** and **Y** on guidelines on the board as you say the stroke descriptions. Use skywriting to model writing **U** and **Y** in the air.

Ask students to use their index finger to trace cursive **U** and **Y** several times in their book. Then model these joinings:
- overcurve-to-undercurve: **Ye**
- undercurve-to-downcurve: **Ud**
- undercurve-to-overcurve: **Un**

2 Practice

Remind students to position their book and grip their pencil correctly for writing.

Ask students to carefully trace the shaded letters with pencil. Then have them write the letters, words, and sentences on the page.

Remind students that when they come to this symbol , they should stop writing and circle their best letter.

3 Evaluate

Tell students it is important to make their writing easy for others to read. Remind them to complete all **Stop and Check** activities. Use the **Better Letters** box on the student page to help students evaluate their cursive **U** and **Y**.

Proper size makes each letter easy to read. Ask:
- Does your **U** fill the space from baseline to headline?
- Does the overcurve stroke in your **Y** cross near the baseline?

School Home Extra Practice
Practice Masters 38–39

Tips From an Occupational Therapist

Have students make their own comic strip. First, have students divide a sheet f paper into four squares. Students should use a ruler to draw a vertical and a horizontal line in the middle of the page. Using a ruler elicits bimanual fine-motor skills and strengthens the fingers of the nondominant hand holding the ruler. Tell students to draw their superhero in the first square, introduce the villain in the second square, draw a battle in the third square, and show the winner in the fourth square.

T67

Review

Objective: To review uppercase cursive **N, M, H, K, U,** and **Y.**

Review Write the names of Native American peoples.

Hopi Yamasee

Kickapoo Natchez Navajo

Huron Maya Yuma Ute

Navajo art is beautiful. Museums have some of it. Young artists make rings. How lovely they are!

Write the paragraph about Navajo art. Remember to begin each sentence with an uppercase letter.

My writing has good ___. □
My writing has good ___. □
My writing has good ___. □
My writing has good ___. □

68

1 Review

Review the stroke descriptions, and model again any letters students might be having difficulty writing. Point out that **N, M, H, K, U,** and **Y** begin with a curve forward stroke.

Ask a volunteer to give a verbal description of one of these letters: **N, M, H, K, U, Y.** Challenge other students to identify the letter being described and then write it on guidelines on the board.

See the **Corrective Strategies** in the Appendix for techniques in correcting common problems in your students' handwriting.

2 Practice

Remind students to position their book and grip their pencil correctly for writing.

Ask students to carefully write the words and paragraph on the page, remembering to form their letters with correct strokes so they will have proper shape.

3 Evaluate

Tell students it is important to make their writing easy for others to read.

Proper Shape, Size, Spacing, and Slant make words easy to read. Ask:

- Did you write with correct strokes so your letters have good shape?
- Did you use the guidelines to write letters with correct size?
- Is there proper space between each letter and word?
- Do your letters with descenders touch the headline of the next writing space?
- Did you write with consistent forward slant?

Digital Resources for Handwriting

Interactive digital resources for whole-class instruction include proper pencil and paper positions for right- and left-handed students, letter animations that show how to form each letter, and letter activities. (Interactive whiteboard compatible.)

Support for English Language Learners

Students might know little about the Native American groups listed on student page 68. Introduce these groups with photos, books, maps, and, if available, videos. Create a class book or a poster of facts about the groups. Write sentence starters, and have students propose ideas to finish the sentences. For example, write, **The Navajo lived in homes called _____.** (*hogans*) If time permits, have students illustrate their work. Note that some students themselves might be indigenous. Have them discuss indigenous groups from their countries.

T68

Read the beginning of the story to the right.

Yuli was from New Mexico, and Heather was from Kansas. The two girls became friends at camp in Utah. One summer, the most exciting thing happened when they went hiking in the Grand Canyon.

On the guidelines below, finish the story by writing what you think happened next. Write in cursive, and remember to leave room for margins.

Stop and Check
Circle your best letter. **69**

Objective: To write a story legibly using cursive handwriting.

1 Review

Read aloud the story starter on student page 69. Review any of the upper- or lowercase letters students might have difficulty with. Call on volunteers to model saying stroke descriptions aloud and writing the letters on the board as students trace them with their index finger on their desk.

Remind students to correctly form **N, M, H, K, U,** and **Y** when they write their story ending.

2 Practice

Remind students to position their book and grip their pencil correctly for writing.

Ask students to carefully write and complete the story starter on the page, remembering to form their letters with correctly written strokes so they will have good shape.

3 Evaluate

Tell students it is important to make their writing easy for others to read. Remind them to complete the **Stop and Check** activity at the end of the lesson.

✓ **Use** these questions to help students evaluate their cursive writing.

- Are your slant strokes pulled toward the baseline?
- Did you use correct strokes so your letters have correct shape?
- Did you remember to dot your **i**'s and cross your **t**'s?

Content Connection *Fine Arts*

Have students choose and research one Native American group that has lived in the area of the Grand Canyon. Ask them to find out the kind of pottery, clothing, artwork, or beading the group made. Have students print pictures that illustrate the group's style of art. Then instruct students to draw their own example of the art form and share it with the class.

T69

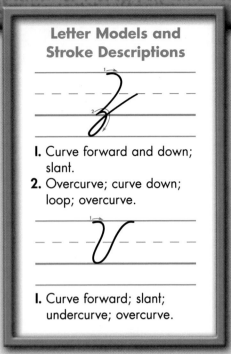

Letter Models and Stroke Descriptions

1. Curve forward and down; slant.
2. Overcurve; curve down; loop; overcurve.

1. Curve forward; slant; undercurve; overcurve.

Objective: To practice and master uppercase cursive **Z** and **V**.

Write Curve Forward Letters
Trace and write.

Find a curve forward stroke in each letter.

Joining Alert! Z is joined to the letter that follows, but V is not.

Write the words and sentences.

Zoe   Zelda   Victor   Vera

Violins have four strings.

Zithers have strings also.

Better Letters
Start Z and V with a curve forward stroke.
Write: Z not z V not V

Use your best handwriting to write the letters again.

Stop and Check
Circle your best Z and your best V.

70

---

1 Model

Talk about cursive **Z** and **V**. Ask:
- How many loops are in **Z**? *(one)*
- How does **V** end? *(with an overcurve)*

Write cursive **Z** and **V** on guidelines on the board as you say the stroke descriptions. Use skywriting (see Appendix) to model writing **Z** and then **V** in the air.

Ask students to use their index finger to trace cursive **Z** and **V** in their book. Then model these joinings:
- overcurve-to-undercurve: **Ze**
- overcurve-to-downcurve: **Za**
- overcurve-to-overcurve: **Zy**

School Home Extra Practice
Practice Masters 40–41

2 Practice

Remind students to
- position their book on the tabletop correctly for writing; and
- grip their pencil correctly for writing.

Ask students to carefully trace the shaded letters with pencil. Then have them write the letters, words, and sentences on the page.

Remind students that when they come to this symbol ✓, they should stop writing and circle their best letter.

3 Evaluate

Tell students it is important to make their writing easy for others to read. Remind them to complete all **Stop and Check** activities, including the one at the end of the lesson.

✓ Use the **Better Letters** box on student page 70 and these questions to help students evaluate their cursive **Z** and **V**:
- Is your **Z** about the same width as the model?
- Did you leave the correct amount of space between **V** and the next letter in the word?

Support for
English Language Learners

Write several words that begin with **z** or **Z** on the board. Examples: **zebra, zipper, zero, zone, Zeke, Zelda**. Explain that the letter **z** is not a commonly used letter in English. Ask students about **Z** in their first language. Is it common? Remind students that the letter **z** sounds like "zeeee." Say each word as you skywrite uppercase **Z** in the air. Have students say the words along with you.

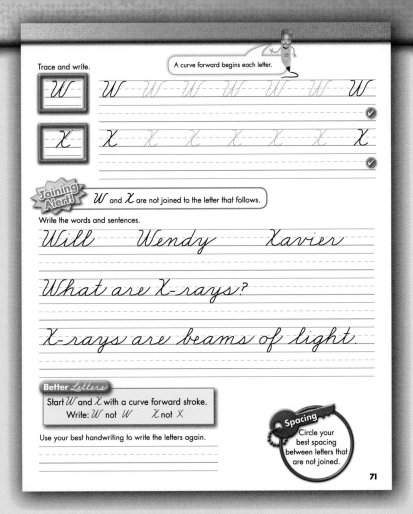

Trace and write.

A curve forward begins each letter.

$\mathcal{W}$ $\mathcal{W}$ $\mathcal{W}$ $\mathcal{W}$ $\mathcal{W}$ $\mathcal{W}$ $\mathcal{W}$ $\mathcal{W}$

$\mathcal{X}$ $\mathcal{X}$ $\mathcal{X}$ $\mathcal{X}$ $\mathcal{X}$ $\mathcal{X}$ $\mathcal{X}$ $\mathcal{X}$

Joining Alert! $\mathcal{W}$ and $\mathcal{X}$ are not joined to the letter that follows.

Write the words and sentences.

Will   Wendy   Xavier

What are X-rays?

X-rays are beams of light.

Better Letters
Start $\mathcal{W}$ and $\mathcal{X}$ with a curve forward stroke.
Write: $\mathcal{W}$ not $\mathcal{W}$ $\mathcal{X}$ not $\mathcal{X}$

Use your best handwriting to write the letters again.

Spacing Circle your best spacing between letters that are not joined.

71

Letter Models and Stroke Descriptions

1. Curve forward; slant; undercurve.
2. Slant; undercurve; overcurve.

1. Curve forward; slant; undercurve. Lift.
2. Slant.

Objective: To practice and master uppercase cursive **W** and **X**.

---

1 Model

Talk about cursive **W** and **X**. Ask:
- How many undercurves does **W** have? *(two)*
- What kind of joining letter is **X**? *(It does not join to the letter that follows.)*

Write cursive **W** and **X** on guidelines on the board as you say the stroke descriptions. Emphasize that **W** and **X** do not join the letters that follow. Use skywriting to model writing **W** and **X** in the air. Have students stand and say the stroke descriptions with you as they write cursive **W** and **X** in the air.

Ask students to use their finger to trace **W** and **X** several times in their book.

2 Practice

Remind students to position their book and grip their pencil correctly for writing.

Ask students to carefully trace the shaded letters with pencil. Then have them write the letters, words, and sentences on the page.

Remind students that when they come to this symbol ✓, they should stop writing and circle their best letter.

3 Evaluate

Tell students it is important to make their writing easy for others to read. Remind them to complete all **Stop and Check** activities. Use the **Better Letters** box to help students evaluate **W** and **X**.

Proper spacing makes each letter easy to read. Ask:
- Did you leave the correct amount of spacing between letters?
- Are your letters neither too far apart nor too close together?

School Home Extra Practice
Practice Masters 42–43

Writing Center

Have students work in small groups to research X-rays. They can use resource books or the Internet to write answers to one or more of these questions: *What are X-rays? What do X-rays do? Why do people or animals occasionally need to have X-rays?* Encourage groups to elect a leader to present their findings to the class. (Internet use should be carefully monitored).

T71

Review

Objective: To review uppercase cursive **Z, V, W,** and **X**.

Review

Write the names of inventors.

Vladimir Zworykin

George Washington Carver

Wilbur and Orville Wright

Wheels turn on axles.
X-rays show bones.
Zippers fasten jackets.
Velcro holds things together.

Write the sentences about inventions. Begin each sentence with an uppercase letter.

72

1 Review

Review the stroke descriptions, and model any letters students might be having difficulty writing. Point out that letters **Z, V, W,** and **X** all contain a curve forward stroke.

Ask a volunteer to give a verbal description of one of these letters: **Z, V, W,** or **X**. Challenge the other students to identify the letter being described and write it on guidelines on the board.

See the **Corrective Strategies** in the Appendix for techniques in correcting common problems in your students' handwriting.

2 Practice

Remind students to position their book and grip their pencil correctly for writing.

Ask students to carefully write the names of the inventors on the page, remembering to form their letters with correct strokes so they will have proper shape.

3 Evaluate

Tell students it is important to make their writing easy for others to read.

✓ **Use** these questions to help students evaluate their cursive writing:

- Did you write with correct strokes so your letters have good shape?
- Did you remember to dot your **i**'s and cross your **t**'s?
- Did you use the guidelines to write letters with correct size?
- Did you follow the models for good spacing in your writing?

▶ Digital Resources for Handwriting

Interactive digital resources for whole-class instruction include proper pencil and paper positions for right- and left-handed students, letter animations that show how to form each letter, and letter activities. (Interactive whiteboard compatible.)

Support for English Language Learners

Because sentence word order is different in different languages, some students might need additional help with the order of words in a sentence. Write the words **subject-verb** on the board. Use the four sentences on student page 72 to help students identify the subject and the verb. Then read the sentences aloud. Have students read the sentences aloud after you. Encourage students to compare the English word order with the order in their first language.

T72

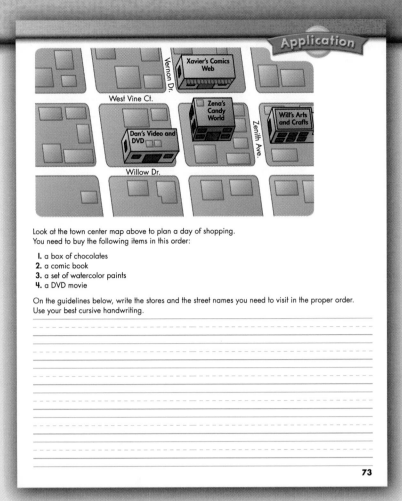

Application

Look at the town center map above to plan a day of shopping.
You need to buy the following items in this order:

1. a box of chocolates
2. a comic book
3. a set of watercolor paints
4. a DVD movie

On the guidelines below, write the stores and the street names you need to visit in the proper order.
Use your best cursive handwriting.

73

Application

Objective: To use a town center map to write store and street names.

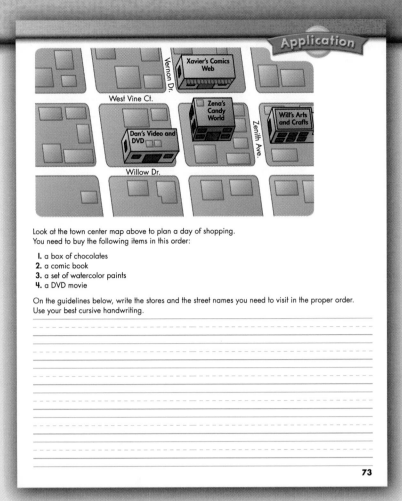

1 Review

Have students look at the town center map on student page 73. Say the names of the stores and the streets. Read aloud the directions and the list of items to buy on the student page.

Remind students to correctly form cursive **Z, V, W,** and **X** when they write the names of the stores and the streets.

2 Practice

Remind students to position their book and grip their pencil correctly for writing.

Ask students to carefully write the stores and street names that they need to visit in proper order on the page. Remind students to form their letters with carefully written strokes so they will have proper shape.

3 Evaluate

Tell students it is important to make their writing easy for others to read.

Proper Shape, Size, Spacing, and Slant make words easy to read. Ask:

- Are your slant strokes pulled toward the baseline?
- Is there proper space between each letter and word?
- Do your letters look like the models?
- Did you use proper slant?

Tips From an
Occupational Therapist

Provide a large puzzle on a table as a fine-motor activity for students to choose during free time. Manipulating the pieces requires individual finger movement, while finding the appropriate spot for each piece requires a high degree of visual perceptual skills.

T73

Letter Models and Stroke Descriptions

1. Overcurve; curve down and up.
2. Retrace; curve right.

1. Overcurve; slant; loop back; overcurve.

1. Curve back; overcurve; curve down; retrace; curve forward; curve under.

Objective: To practice and master uppercase cursive **I, J,** and **Q.**

Write Overcurve Letters
Trace and write.

Find an overcurve in each letter.

Joining Alert! J is joined to the letter that follows, but I and Q are not.

Write the names.

Inez   Justin   Quinn

Isabella   Jackie   Quincy

Better Letters

Write: I not I, J not J, Q not Q

Use your best handwriting to write the letters again.

Stop and Check
Circle your best I, your best J, and your best Q.

74

---

1 Model

Talk about cursive **I, J,** and **Q.** Ask:
- Where do **I** and **J** begin? *(just below the baseline)*
- How does **Q** begin? *(with a curve back, overcurve)*

Write I, J, and **Q** on guidelines on the board as you say the stroke descriptions.

Remind students that **I** and **Q** are not joined to the letter that follows. Then model these joinings:
- overcurve-to-undercurve: **Je**
- overcurve-to-downcurve: **Ja**

2 Practice

Remind students to
- position their book on the tabletop correctly for writing; and
- grip their pencil correctly for writing.

Ask students to carefully trace the shaded letters with pencil. Then have them write the letters and words on the page.

Remind students that when they come to this symbol ✓, they should stop writing and circle their best letter.

3 Evaluate

Tell students it is important to make their writing easy for others to read. Remind them to complete all **Stop and Check** activities, including the one at the bottom of the page.

✓ **Use** the **Better Letters** box on the student page and these questions to help students evaluate their cursive **I, J,** and **Q:**
- Does your **I** have good slant?
- Does your **J** begin just below the baseline?
- Is your **Q** about the same width as the model?

School Home Extra Practice
Practice Masters 44–46

Support for
English Language Learners

Write the letters **I, J,** and **Q** on the board. Point to each letter and have students name a person or place, in English or in their first launguage, that begins with that letter. Write their words on the board. Say the words and have students say them after you.

T74

Write Doublecurve Letters

Trace and write.

There is a doublecurve in each letter.

Joining Alert! $\mathcal{T}$ and $\mathcal{F}$ are not joined to the letter that follows.

Write the names and sentences.

Tara Tim Fiona Finn

Forests keep us healthy.

Their leaves make oxygen.

Better Letters

Lift after the curve forward and right stroke.
Write: $\mathcal{T}$ not $\mathcal{T}$ $\mathcal{F}$ not $\mathcal{F}$

Use your best handwriting to write the letters again.

Slant Circle three words you wrote that have good slant.

75

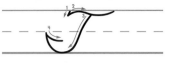

Letter Models and Stroke Descriptions

1. Slant.
2. Curve forward and right. Lift.
3. Doublecurve; curve up.
4. Retrace; curve right.

1. Slant.
2. Curve forward and right. Lift.
3. Doublecurve; curve up.
4. Retrace; curve right. Lift.
5. Slide right.

Objective: To practice and master uppercase cursive **T** and **F**.

---

1 Model

Talk about cursive **T** and **F**. Ask:
- Where do **T** and **F** begin? *(at the headline)*
- How are **T** and **F** different from each other? *(F has a final slide right stroke.)*

Write cursive **T** and **F** on guidelines on the board as you say the stroke descriptions. Ask students to use their index finger to trace **T** and **F** several times in their book.

Remind students that **T** and **F** are not joined to the letter that follows.

2 Practice

Remind students to position their book and grip their pencil correctly for writing.

Ask students to carefully trace the shaded letters with pencil. Then have them write the letters, words, and sentences on the page.

Remind students that when they come to this symbol ✓, they should stop writing and circle their best letter.

3 Evaluate

Tell students it is important to make their writing easy for others to read. Remind them to complete all **Stop and Check** activities.

✓ **Use** the **Better Letters** box on student page 75 and these questions to help students evaluate their **T** and **F**.

Proper slant makes each letter easy to read. Ask:
- Did you position your book properly for writing?
- Do your cursive letters have uniform forward slant?

School Home Extra Practice
Practice Masters 47–48

 **Content Connection** **Science**

Have students work in pairs to research fun facts about trees in their area or in their state. They can use resource books or the Internet to locate information about trees. Have students write a paragraph in cursive about the tree they chose to research. Encourage them to include an illustration. (Internet use should be carefully monitored.)

T75

Review

Objective: To review uppercase cursive **I, J, Q, T,** and **F**.

Review

Write the names of coastal cities.

Iwaki, Japan

Tocopilla, Chile

Qingdao, China

Tsunamis are huge waves. Floods come if one hits. I saw one once on television. Japan has tsunamis.

Write the paragraph. Begin each sentence with an uppercase letter. Leave room for margins.

76

---

1 Review

Review the stroke descriptions, and model any letters students might be having difficulty writing. Point out that **I, J,** and **Q** contain an overcurve stroke, and **T** and **F** contain a double-curve stroke.

Ask a volunteer to give a verbal description of one of these letters: **I, J, Q, T,** or **F**. Challenge the other students to identify the letter being described and write it on guidelines on the board.

See the **Corrective Strategies** in the Appendix for techniques in correcting common problems in your students' handwriting.

Digital Resources for Handwriting

Interactive digital resources for whole-class instruction include proper pencil and paper positions for right- and left-handed students, letter animations that show how to form each letter, and letter activities. (Interactive whiteboard compatible.)

2 Practice

Remind students to position their book and grip their pencil correctly for writing.

Have students read the directions and carefully write the names of coastal cities on student page 76. Then have them write the paragraph about tsunamis at the bottom of the page, remembering to form their letters with correct strokes so they will have proper shape, size, spacing, and slant. Remind students to leave room for margins.

3 Evaluate

Tell students it is important to make their writing easy for others to read.

✅ **Use** these questions to help students evaluate their cursive writing:

- Are your slant strokes pulled toward the baseline?
- Is there proper space between each letter and word?
- Do your letters look like the models?
- Did you use proper slant?

Support for
English Language Learners

Some students might need help with the pronunciation of the words on student page 76. Write the words **Iwaki, Tocopilla, Qingdao,** and **tsunamis** on the board. Next to each word, write the words divided into syllables and as they are pronounced: **I•wa•kee, To•co•pil•la, Quing•da•o,** and **tsoo•na•me**. Say the words aloud and have students repeat them after you. Discuss the location or meaning of each word.

T76

Listed below are some famous landmarks and their locations.

Niagara Falls: New York	Mount Rushmore: South Dakota
Hoover Dam: Nevada	Kennedy Space Center: Florida
United States Capitol: Washington, D.C.	Yosemite National Park: California

Write the name of the famous place you would see in each city or state. Use your best cursive writing.

Visit South Dakota to see

Visit New York to see

Visit California to see

Visit Washington, D.C. to see

Visit Nevada to see

Visit Florida to see

77

Objective: To use names of states to write famous places.

1 Review

Discuss with students the names in the list of famous places and their locations. Use a map of the United States to point out each state. Read aloud the directions on student page 77.

Remind students to use their best cursive handwriting.

2 Practice

Remind students to position their book and grip their pencil correctly for writing.

Ask students to carefully write the name of the famous place they would see in each state, remembering to form their letters with carefully written strokes so they will have proper shape, size, spacing, and slant.

3 Evaluate

Tell students it is important to make their writing easy for others to read. Proper Shape, Size, Spacing, and Slant make words easy to read. Ask:

- Did you write with correct strokes so your letters have good shape?
- Did you use the guidelines to make letters with correct size?
- Did you follow the models so your writing has good spacing?
- Does your writing have consistent forward slant?

Writing Center

Pair students and ask them to use manuscript writing to create a word-search puzzle for classmates to solve. Have them use several of the famous places and their locations on student page 77.

T77

Letter Models and Stroke Descriptions

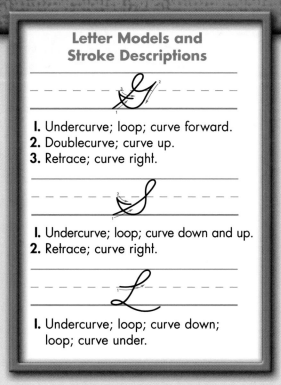

1. Undercurve; loop; curve forward.
2. Doublecurve; curve up.
3. Retrace; curve right.

1. Undercurve; loop; curve down and up.
2. Retrace; curve right.

1. Undercurve; loop; curve down; loop; curve under.

Objective: To practice and master uppercase cursive **G, S,** and **L**.

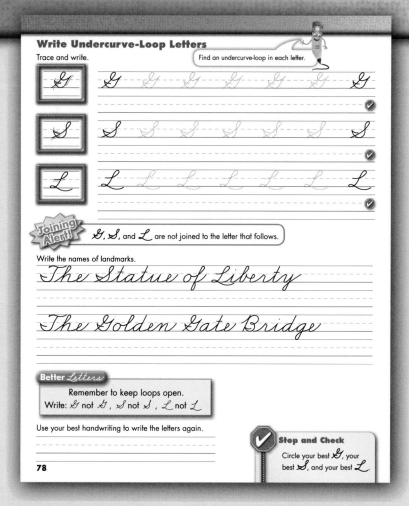

Write Undercurve-Loop Letters
Trace and write.

Find an undercurve-loop in each letter.

Joining Alert! G, S, and L are not joined to the letter that follows.

Write the names of landmarks.

The Statue of Liberty

The Golden Gate Bridge

Better Letters
Remember to keep loops open.
Write: G not G, S not S, L not L

Use your best handwriting to write the letters again.

78

Stop and Check
Circle your best G, your best S, and your best L.

---

1 Model

Talk about cursive **G, S,** and **L**. Ask:
- Where does **G** begin? (*at the baseline*)
- How many loops are in **S**? (*one*)
- Where does **L** end? (*just below the baseline*)

Write cursive **G, S,** and **L** on guidelines on the board as you say the stroke descriptions. Use skywriting (see Appendix) to model writing the letters in the air.

Tell students that the letters **G, S,** and **L** are not joined to the letter that follows.

 **Extra Practice**
Practice Masters 49–51

2 Practice

Remind students to
- position their book on the tabletop correctly for writing; and
- grip their pencil correctly for writing.

Ask students to carefully trace the shaded letters with pencil. Then have them write the letters and the words on the page.

Remind students that when they come to this symbol ✓, they should stop writing and circle their best letter.

3 Evaluate

Tell students it is important to make their writing easy for others to read. Remind them to complete all **Stop and Check** activities, including the one at the bottom of the page.

✓ **Use** the **Better Letters** box on the student page and these questions to help students evaluate their cursive **G, S,** and **L**:
- Is your **G** about the same width as the model?
- Does your **S** have good slant?
- Does your **L** begin at the midline?

Support for
English Language Learners

Write several words that begin with **g** or **G** on the board. Examples: **game, gem, giant,** and **Golden Gate**. Explain that the letter **g** can have the /g/ sound as well as other sounds. For example, it can have a "hard sound" of **g** as in *gate*, a "soft sound" of **g** as in *gem*, and the /j/ sound as in *giant*. Say each word aloud, and help students determine the sound the letter **g** makes in each word. Encourage them to identify words in their first language that begin with **g** or **G**.

T78

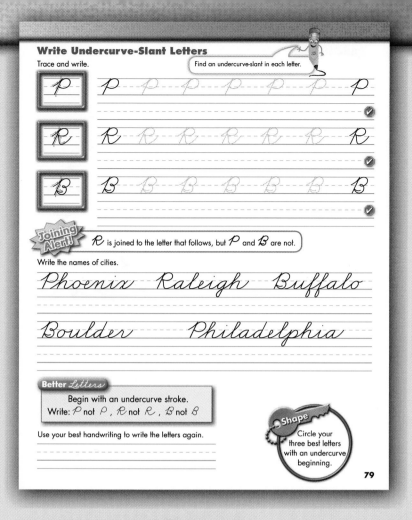

Write Undercurve-Slant Letters

Trace and write.

Find an undercurve-slant in each letter.

(handwriting practice rows for P, R, B)

Joining Alert! $\mathcal{R}$ is joined to the letter that follows, but $\mathcal{P}$ and $\mathcal{B}$ are not.

Write the names of cities.

Phoenix   Raleigh   Buffalo

Boulder   Philadelphia

Better *Letters*

Begin with an undercurve stroke.
Write: $\mathcal{P}$ not P , $\mathcal{R}$ not R , $\mathcal{B}$ not B

Use your best handwriting to write the letters again.

Shape Circle your three best letters with an undercurve beginning.

79

Letter Models and Stroke Descriptions

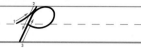

1. Undercurve.
2. Slant.
3. Retrace; curve forward and back.

1. Undercurve.
2. Slant.
3. Retrace; curve forward and back.
4. Curve forward; undercurve.

1. Undercurve.
2. Slant.
3. Retrace; curve forward; loop; curve forward and back.
4. Retrace; curve right.

Objective: To practice and master uppercase cursive **P, R,** and **B.**

---

1 Model

Talk about cursive **P, R,** and **B.** Ask:
- How does **P** begin? *(with an undercurve)*
- Which letter has a loop? *(B)*
- Where is the retrace in **R**? *(after the slant)*

Write cursive **P, R,** and **B** on guidelines on the board as you say the stroke descriptions. Model writing **P, R,** and **B** in the air. Have students stand and say the stroke descriptions with you as they skywrite cursive **P, R,** and **B** in the air.

Tell students that **R** is joined to the letter that follows, but **P** and **B** are not.

2 Practice

Remind students to position their book and grip their pencil correctly for writing.

Ask students to carefully trace the shaded letters with pencil. Then have them write the letters and words on the page.

Remind students that when they come to this symbol ✓, they should stop writing and circle their best letter.

3 Evaluate

Tell students it is important to make their writing easy for others to read. Remind them to complete all **Stop and Check** activities.
Use the **Better Letters** box on the student page to help students evaluate their **P, R,** and **B.**

Proper shape makes each letter easy to read. Ask:
- Is your **P** closed?
- Does your **R** begin at the midline?
- Does your **B** have good slant?

School Home **Extra Practice**
Practice Masters 52–54

Tips From an
Occupational Therapist

Organize students into pairs and provide each pair with a tennis ball. Instruct them to bounce the ball to one another. Then tell students to catch the ball with their left hand, pass it to their right hand behind their back, and then bounce it back to their partner. This gross-motor activity helps students develop hand-eye coordination and upper-extremity dexterity and helps maintain the arches of the hand.

T79

Review

Objective: To review uppercase cursive **G, S, L, P, R,** and **B.**

1 Review

Review the stroke descriptions, and model any letters students might be having difficulty writing. Point out that letters **G, S,** and **L** contain an under-curve-loop stroke while **P, R,** and **B** begin with a undercurve-slant stroke.

Ask volunteers to give a verbal description of one of these letters: **G, S, L, P, R,** or **B.** Challenge the other students to identify the letter being described and write it on guidelines on the board.

See the **Corrective Strategies** in the Appendix for techniques in correcting common problems in your students' handwriting.

2 Practice

Remind students to position their book and grip their pencil correctly for writing.

Have students read the directions and carefully write the names of baseball teams on student page 80. Then have them write the list of baseball equipment at the bottom of the page, remembering to form their letters with correct strokes so they will have proper shape, size, spacing, and slant. Remind students to leave space for margins.

3 Evaluate

Tell students it is important to make their writing easy for others to read.

✓ **Use** these questions to help students evaluate their cursive writing:

- Are your slant strokes pulled toward the baseline?
- Is there proper space between each letter and word?
- Do your letters look like the models?
- Did you use proper slant?

▶ Digital Resources for Handwriting

Interactive digital resources for whole-class instruction include proper pencil and paper positions for right- and left-handed students, letter animations that show how to form each letter, and letter activities. (Interactive whiteboard compatible.)

Support for English Language Learners

Some students might not be familiar with the pieces of equipment that should be used when playing baseball. Poll students to find out how many wear helmets when they play baseball and ask why helmets are important to wear. Then call attention to the shin guards. Ask volunteers to describe why they think shin guards are important pieces of baseball safety equipment. Have students write a sentence about baseball. Encourage them to compare the equipment items to a sport in their native country or to a sport they know.

This timeline is out of order. Write the dates and events in the proper order below. Use your best cursive handwriting.

Professional Baseball Timeline

1903	1947	1876	1974	1900	1935
Boston and Pittsburgh play first World Series.	Jackie Robinson is first African American in majors.	National League is formed.	Hank Aaron breaks Babe Ruth's home run record.	American League is formed.	George Herman "Babe" Ruth hits final home run.

81

Objective: To write a timeline using legible cursive handwriting.

1 Review

Discuss with students the players named in the timeline. Encourage students to share what they know about the players and the important baseball dates on student page 81. Then look at the timeline. Invite a volunteer to explain what the purpose of a timeline is. Read aloud the directions and the timeline events.

Remind students to use their best cursive writing and leave room for margins.

2 Practice

Remind students to position their book and grip their pencil correctly for writing.

Ask students to carefully write the dates and events in the proper order, remembering to form their letters with carefully written strokes so they have proper shape, size, spacing, and slant.

3 Evaluate

Tell students it is important to make their writing easy for others to read.

Proper Shape, Size, Spacing, and Slant make words easy to read. Ask:

- Did you write with correct strokes so your letters have good shape?
- Did you use the guidelines to help you write letters with correct size?
- Did you follow the models so your writing has good spacing?
- Does your writing have consistent forward slant?

Content Connection — Social Studies

Have students make a personal timeline of important events in their lives. Discuss general milestone ideas for their timelines, such as date of birth, first year of school, a sports event, a special vacation or family event, or the arrival of younger siblings or a family pet. Suggest they use the timeline on student page 81 as a model. Invite students to share their timelines with a classmate or with the whole class.

T81

Keys to Legibility

Shape 🗝️
describes the strokes that form each letter and give it a unique appearance.

Size 🗝️
describes the height of letters.

Spacing 🗝️
describes the space between letters, words, and sentences.

Slant 🗝️
describes the angle of writing on the paper.

Objective: To practice the four Keys to Legibility.

Keys to Legibility

My favorite team is the Green Bay Packers. My brother Levi likes the Saint Louis Rams. My sister Gwen doesn't agree with either of us. She is a Chicago Bears fan. But we all think that football is the best sport ever!

82

Handwriting Coach

Keys to Legibility Explain to students that good handwriting is legible handwriting. Review with students the qualities of legible handwriting. Write their responses on the board. These might include neatness, carefully written letters, and letters that are not too crowded.

Point out that the four Keys to Legibility are easy to remember because they all start with **s**: **Shape, Size, Spacing,** and **Slant**.

Explain that **Shape** describes the strokes that form each letter and give it a unique appearance. **Size** describes the height of letters. **Spacing** describes the space between letters, words, and sentences. **Slant** refers to the angle of writing on the paper. Tell students that using these Keys will help them improve the legibility of their writing.

1 Review

Read and discuss with students the photograph on student page 82. Then read aloud the paragraph about football teams on the student page.

2 Practice

Read the directions on student page 83. Remind students to focus on the four Keys to Legibility—Shape, Size, Spacing, and Slant—as they write the paragraph about football teams. Emphasize that their writing should be easy to read. Remind them to leave space for margins.

Support for
English Language Learners

Have students look at the Keys to Legibility booklet they prepared to review the four Keys: shape, size, spacing, and slant. Ask students to discuss why shape, size, spacing, and slant are necessary tools in learning and practicing handwriting. Have students write additional words on each of the four pages in their Keys to Legibility booklet, either in English or in their native language. That will help them remember the importance of each Key.

T82

Write the paragraph about football teams.
Make your writing easy to read. Be sure to leave space for margins.

Is your writing easy to read?

Shape
Circle your best letter that has an undercurve-loop beginning.

Size
Circle your best tall letter.

Spacing
Circle two words that have space for \ between them.

Slant
Circle a word you wrote that has good slant.

83

3 Evaluate

Tell students it is important to make their writing easy for others to read.

Shape
- Does each letter have its own clear shape?
- Did you end each short undercurve stroke near the midline?
- Did you end each tall undercurve stroke near the headline?

Size
- Did you use the guidelines to write letters with correct size?
- Do your tall letters touch the headline and the baseline?
- Are short letters the same height?

Spacing
- Are your letters neither too close together nor too far apart?
- Is there space for O between letters in your words?
- Is there space for \ between your words?

Slant
- Does your writing have uniform forward slant?
- Did you pull your downstrokes in the proper direction?
- Is your writing easy to read?

Writing Center

Ask students to write about an excursion they took to a place of interest in their community. Encourage them to share their story with a classmate or the entire class.

Uppercase Review

Objective: To review and practice writing all the uppercase cursive letters.

Uppercase Review

Write downcurve letters.

A O D C E

Write curve forward letters.

N M H K U Y Z V W X

Write overcurve letters.

I J Q

Write doublecurve letters.

T F

Write undercurve-loop letters.

G S L

Write undercurve-slant letters.

P R B

Write the names of cities.

Ithaca Tulsa Seattle

Baltimore Dallas Xenia

84

1 Review

Review the stroke descriptions, and model any letters students might be having difficulty writing. Point out that all the uppercase letters on student page 84 are grouped according to the strokes they contain.

Ask a volunteer to give a verbal description of one of the letters from one of the six groupings. Challenge the other students to identify the letter being described and write it on guidelines on the board.

See the **Corrective Strategies** in the Appendix for techniques in correcting common problems in your students' handwriting.

2 Practice

Remind students to position their book and grip their pencil correctly for writing.

Have students write the uppercase letters within each group and the names of the cities on student page 84, remembering to form their letters with correct strokes so they will have proper shape, size, spacing, and slant.

3 Evaluate

Tell students it is important to make their writing easy for others to read.

✅ **Use** these questions to help students evaluate their cursive writing:

- Did you write with correct strokes so your letters have good shape?
- Did you use the guidelines to write letters with correct size?
- Did you use good spacing between your letters and your words?
- Does your writing have uniform forward slant?

Support for
English Language Learners

Some students might need help with the pronunciation of the cities at the bottom of the page. Write the words **Ithaca, Tulsa, Seattle, Baltimore, Dallas,** and **Xenia** on the board. Say the words aloud and have students repeat them after you. Use a map of the United States to point out the state in which each of the cities is located. *(Ithaca, New York; Tulsa, Oklahoma; Seattle, Washington; Baltimore, Maryland; Dallas, Texas; Xenia, Ohio)*

Joining Alert!

Remember! These letters are joined to the letter that follows.

A C E H J K M N R U Y Z

These letters are not.

B D F G I L O P Q S T V W X

Write these song titles. Remember to use quotation marks.

"America the Beautiful"

"Yankee Doodle"

"Texas, Our Texas"

"This Land Is Your Land"

"Georgia on My Mind"

"Hawaii Ponoi"

85

1 Review

Discuss with students the text in the **Joining Alert!** box. Review the group of letters that are joined to the letter that follows and the group of letters that are not joined.

Read aloud the directions and the names of the song titles on student page 85. Ask students to identify which uppercase letters in the song titles are joined to the letter that follows and which are not.

2 Practice

Remind students to position their book and grip their pencil correctly for writing.

Ask students to carefully write the song titles, remembering to form their letters with carefully written strokes so they will have proper shape, size, spacing, and slant. Remind students to use their best cursive writing, leave room for margins, and use quotation marks as they write the song titles.

3 Evaluate

Tell students it is important to make their writing easy for others to read.

✓ **Use** these questions to help students evaluate their cursive writing:

- Did you write using correct joining strokes?
- Did you use the guidelines to write letters with correct size?
- Did you use good spacing between letters in words and between words?
- Does your writing have uniform forward slant?

Tips From an
Occupational Therapist

To increase fine-motor dexterity, have students do paper weaving. First have students create a paper loom by folding a thick piece of construction paper in half horizontally. Tell them to use scissors to cut vertical lines every 1–2 inches along the folded edge of the paper. Then have students cut out paper strips and weave them through the openings of the paper loom.

Objective: To evaluate handwriting progress by writing the same poem written at the beginning of the school year and comparing the two.

It's Dark in Here

I am writing these poems
From inside a lion,
And it's rather dark in here.
So please excuse the handwriting
Which may not be too clear.
But this afternoon by the lion's cage
I'm afraid I got too near.
And I'm writing these lines
From inside a lion,
And it's rather dark in here.

by Shel Silverstein

86

Handwriting Coach

Keys to Legibility

Remind students to use the four Keys to Legibility—Shape, Size, Spacing, and Slant—as a rubric for evaluating their handwriting.

1 Review

Remind students that at the beginning of the school year they wrote this poem as a pretest and evaluated their handwriting. Read the poem aloud with students. Then point out the writing space on student page 87, where they are to write the poem again.

2 Posttest

Ask students to write the poem using their best cursive handwriting. As they write the poem in cursive as a posttest, remind them to use correct letter shape and size, correct spacing, and uniform slant.

Support for
English Language Learners

Help students develop the skill of self-evaluation by identifying error patterns that will be easy for them to recognize. For example, you might notice that a student consistently omits end punctuation. Work with that student to gauge his or her awareness of this error pattern. You might have the student read his or her writing aloud to you. If the student stops reading when he or she detects an error, that student will more easily incorporate correction strategies than will a student who reads past errors. For students who read past their errors, model the self-evaluation process with individuals or small groups.

T86

Write the poem in your best cursive handwriting.

Is your writing easy to read?   Yes   No

Write your five best cursive letters.

Write five cursive letters you would like to improve.

87

Evaluate

Have students use the Keys to Legibility to evaluate their handwriting. Ask them to respond to the evaluation information at the bottom of student page 87. Then suggest that they compare this writing with their writing on the pretest on student page 9 and discuss how their writing has changed. Meet individually with students to help them assess their progress.

Note: Zaner-Bloser's *Evaluation Guide* for Grade 4 is a handy tool for evaluating students' writing. The evaluation criteria are the Keys to Legibility. Samples of students' handwriting, ranging in quality from excellent to poor, provide a helpful comparison for evaluation.

Content Connection

Ask students to reflect on the meaning of the poem by Shel Silverstein. Ask them why the speaker in the poem says his handwriting is not clear *(It's dark because he is inside a lion)*. Discuss how lighting, posture, and hand position affect the neatness of their writing. Then point out how poetry can say things in a clever, funny, and artful way. Ask students to write a short poem about handwriting.

Handwriting Coach

Evaluation

Self-evaluation is an important step in the handwriting process. By identifying their own strengths and weaknesses, students become independent learners. The steps in the self-evaluation process are as follows:

Question Students should ask themselves questions such as these: "Is my slant correct?" "Do my letters rest on the baseline?" Teacher modeling is vital in teaching effective questioning techniques.

Compare Students should compare their handwriting to correct models.

Evaluate Students should determine strengths and weaknesses in their handwriting based on the Keys to Legibility.

Diagnose Students should diagnose the cause of any difficulties. Possible causes include incorrect paper or pencil position, inconsistent pressure on the writing implement, and incorrect strokes.

Improve Self-evaluation should include a means of improvement through additional instruction and continued practice.

T87

Background Information

Fear of the dark is a common phobia among children. People can't see well in the dark, and children with active imaginations often worry about what might be lurking in the shadows. One way of helping children combat this fear is to have them sleep with a doll, a special blanket, or another item (such as a picture or a poem) that brings them a feeling of comfort and security.

Objective: To read a poem and discuss its meaning.

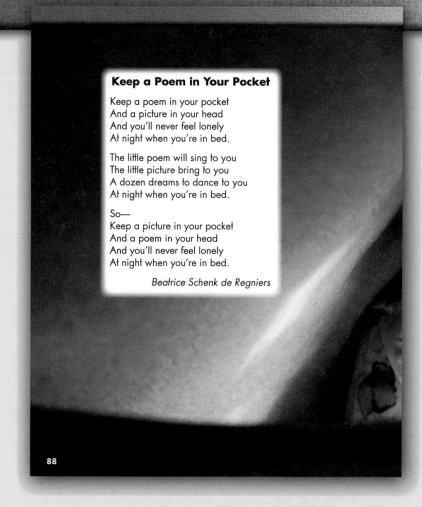

Keep a Poem in Your Pocket

Keep a poem in your pocket
And a picture in your head
And you'll never feel lonely
At night when you're in bed.

The little poem will sing to you
The little picture bring to you
A dozen dreams to dance to you
At night when you're in bed.

So—
Keep a picture in your pocket
And a poem in your head
And you'll never feel lonely
At night when you're in bed.

Beatrice Schenk de Regniers

88

89

Questions for Discussion

1. How can a poem keep you from feeling lonely?

2. How can a picture keep you from feeling lonely?

3. What does the poet mean by saying "the poem will sing to you"?

4. Which lines are repeated in the poem?

5. Why do you think the poet reversed the words *picture* and *poem* in the last stanza?

Writing Extension

Ask students to think of a time when seeing, hearing, or reading something right before going to bed inspired a dream or nightmare. Have them write a brief description of the dream and the picture, poem, or story that might have triggered it.

T89

Objective: To fill in a Flow Chart using legible manuscript handwriting.

Manuscript Maintenance

Make a Flow Chart
A Flow Chart shows steps in a process. This chart shows how steel is made from iron ore.
Use manuscript to write the steps in order in the Flow Chart. Make your writing fit the space.

Iron Into Steel

4	7	1	6	3	5	2
Oxygen is mixed into the liquid iron.	The steel is made into cars, bridges, trains, and buildings.	Iron ore is mined out of the earth.	The liquid steel cools and hardens into blocks.	At 3,000°F, the iron becomes liquid.	The iron and oxygen change into liquid steel.	The ore is put into a hot furnace.

1.

2.

3.

4.

5.

6.

7.

90

Handwriting Coach

Vertical Slant In order to make manuscript letters vertical, remind students to do the following:

- Use correct paper position.
- Pull the downstrokes in the proper direction.
- Shift the paper as their writing fills the space.

School Home Extra Practice
Practice Masters 56, 61

1 Present the Activity

Explain to students that graphic organizers are ways to display relationships between or among ideas. A Flow Chart is a graphic organizer used to organize information by sequencing the steps in a process.

Read aloud the directions for filling in the Flow Chart on student page 90. Point out the small writing space. Remind students to form their letters with correct strokes so they have proper shape, size, spacing, and slant.

2 Write and Evaluate

Have students read the text for turning iron into steel and carefully write the steps in order on the Flow Chart using their best manuscript handwriting.

✅ **Use** these questions to help students evaluate their writing. Ask:

- Are your basic strokes written correctly?
- Do your letters and numerals fit on the guidelines properly?
- Did you allow correct space in your writing?
- Does all your writing have good vertical slant?

Support for
English Language Learners

Some students might need some extra help with the Flow Chart. Ask students to think about the time and order for getting up in the morning, getting dressed, having breakfast, and leaving for school. Write their responses on the board. Call attention to the order of events. Draw a Flow Chart on the board, and have volunteers fill it in with the steps for getting ready for school. Students may wish to copy the Flow Chart for future reference.

Write for Yourself

Sometimes you write just for yourself. When you write for yourself, you don't have to be as neat as when you write for someone else. But your writing must still be legible. You should be able to read what you have written now and at some future time, too.

For example, you might write a journal entry that is for your eyes only. In the space below, write a journal entry that tells what you did yesterday. Leave space for margins.

Date:

The more you practice writing in cursive, the easier it will be. On the following pages, you will write for yourself by making a schedule and taking notes. You will write in a new, smaller size, too. You will focus on the four Keys to Legibility to help make your writing easy to read.

91

Objective: To write a journal entry using legible handwriting.

1 Present the Activity   2 Write and Evaluate

Tell students that the next few pages have activities that they will be writing for themselves. Explain that they will be writing in a smaller size on new guidelines.

Read and discuss with students the text at the top of page 91. Discuss the different reasons people have for keeping a journal. Emphasize that although their journal entry is private and for their eyes only, their writing should still be legible.

Ask students to write in complete sentences what they did yesterday.

 Use these questions to help students evaluate their writing. Ask:

- Did you form your letters carefully so they are easy to read?
- Did you adjust the size of your writing to fit the new, smaller guidelines?
- Does your writing have good spacing?
- Is your entry written with uniform forward slant?

Handwriting Coach

Sitting Position Correct body position allows students to write smoothly. Encourage students to sit comfortably erect with their feet flat on the floor and their hips touching the back of the chair. Both arms should rest on the desk.

Content Connection Fine Arts

Have students illustrate their journal or diary entry. Tell them to draw a picture of the activities and/or a picture of their personal feelings and thoughts they describe in their entry. Encourage students to use colored pencils, markers, or paints. Start a discussion with students on how their illustrations enhance their journal writing.

Make a Schedule

Objective: To practice writing a schedule using legible cursive handwriting.

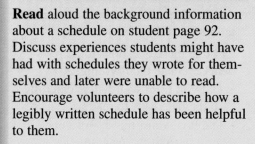

Make a Schedule

Writing a schedule can help you remember things you must do and places you must be. It can also help you remember the order in which you will do things. Here is a schedule:

Monday	4:00	*basketball practice in gym*
	5:00	*help Mom wash Rover*
Tuesday	3:00	*Service Club meeting*
Wednesday		

Add these items to the schedule:

| Tuesday | 8:00 | *surprise party for Grandma* |
| Wednesday | 7:00 | *social studies project with Judy, Kamal, and T'Aysha* |

Collision Alert! Make sure that your tall letters do not bump into the descenders above them.

Size / Shape

| Are your short letters half the height of your tall letters? | Yes | No |
| Do your letters have good shape? | Yes | No |

92

Handwriting Coach

Writing Smaller Before students begin, remind them to adjust their writing to the new handwriting lines and to shift words with ascenders so that ascenders of tall letters do not collide with descenders above them. Provide practice in writing tall letters beneath letters with descenders.

1 Present the Activity

Read aloud the background information about a schedule on student page 92. Discuss experiences students might have had with schedules they wrote for themselves and later were unable to read. Encourage volunteers to describe how a legibly written schedule has been helpful to them.

2 Write and Evaluate

Have students read the directions and complete the activity on student page 92. Point out the **Collision Alert,** and caution students to be aware of "bumping" in their writing.

Correct Shape and Size make writing easy to read. Help students respond to the Key feature at the bottom of the page. Ask:

- Can you see the basic strokes in your letter shapes?
- Do your tall letters fill two-thirds of the writing space?

Support for English Language Learners

Some students might need some extra help with writing a schedule. Ask students to recall filling in a flow chart. Explain that a schedule is similar to a flow chart. It describes in detail activities, appointments, or events on a certain day and time. Write **Day, Time,** and **Activity** on the board. Ask volunteers to fill in the schedule with an activity they will do this week. Suggest that students write their daily schedule and then copy the schedule into a notebook for future reference.

T92

Use cursive to write a schedule of things you might do next week.
Pay attention to the size of your letters.

Monday

Tuesday

Wednesday

Thursday

Friday

Saturday

Size Are your short letters half the height of your tall letters?   Yes   No

93

③ Apply

Ask students to read and follow the directions for writing a schedule of things they might do next week on student page 93. Remind them to write using correct size.

Help students determine whether their writing is legible. Ask them to check that their tall letters don't bump into descenders. Encourage students to practice writing words with tall letters beneath words with descenders, shifting words slightly as necessary.

Correct Size makes writing legible. Help students respond to the Key feature at the bottom of student pages 92 and 93. Ask:

- Are all your short letters the same size?
- Are all your tall letters the same size?
- Did you make sure your tall letters did not bump into descenders?

Handwriting Coach

Size Demonstrate for students the technique of drawing a horizontal line with a ruler along the tops of letters to show proper and consistent size. Have students practice this technique periodically to evaluate their letter size in curriculum areas that require handwriting, especially those that involve writing sentences or paragraphs. Students who have difficulty with proper size of letters should continue to write on paper with a midline and a descender space.

Writing Center

Ask students to make regular entries in a journal. You might begin with a class journal entry about a typical school day and expand to more independent, personal writing. You might wish to share some famous journals and diaries with students. Read excerpts from Henry David Thoreau's journal *Cape Cod* or from *Anne Frank: The Diary of a Young Girl*.

T93

Take Notes

Before Writing

Before students begin, remind them to adjust their writing to the new handwriting lines. Help them group the letters according to size, and provide opportunities to practice proper placement of each letter on the handwriting lines.

- Tall letters should not touch the headline. Lowercase **b, d, f, h, k, l,** and **t** are tall. All uppercase letters are tall.
- Short letters are half the size of tall letters. Lowercase **a, c, e, g, i, j, m, n, o, p, q, r, s, u, v, w, x, y,** and **z** are short.
- Letters with descenders extend below the baseline. Lowercase **f, g, j, p, q, y,** and **z** have descenders. Uppercase **J, Y,** and **Z** have descenders.

Objective: To practice taking notes using legible cursive handwriting.

Take Notes

When you take notes from a book, write the title and the author. Then write the important facts in your own words.

Flight! by Harry Roberts
1804— Sir George Cayley builds and flies first successful glider
1896— Samuel P. Langley flies model of a steam-powered airplane over Potomac River
1900–1903— Orville and Wilbur Wright build and test glider

Write the notes. Try to write quickly, but make sure your writing is still legible.

My writing has good ☐
My writing has good ☐
My writing has good ☐
My writing has good ☐

94

---

1 Present the Activity

Read aloud the background information about taking notes on student page 94. Discuss experiences students might have had with notes they wrote for themselves and later were unable to read. Encourage volunteers to describe how legibly written notes have been helpful to them.

2 Write and Evaluate

Have students read the directions and complete the activity on student page 94.

Help students as needed to complete the activity on the page.

Use these questions to help students evaluate their writing:

- Are your slant strokes pulled toward the baseline?
- Is there proper space between each letter and word?
- Do your letters look like the models?
- Did you use proper slant?

Support for
English Language Learners

Some students might need help with the pronunciation of the names and places on student page 94. Use pictures or illustrations to show the history of flight. Write the names **Harry Roberts, Sir George Cayley, Samuel P. Langley, Potomac River,** and **Orville** and **Wilbur Wright** on the board. Say each name, placing emphasis on the stressed syllable. Then have students say the names after you. Finally, have students write a sentence about flight.

T94

Take notes from the following paragraph.
Make your writing easy to read.

Flight! by Harry Roberts

On December 17, 1903, Orville and Wilbur Wright flew their plane in Kitty Hawk, North Carolina, four times. The soil was sandy and soft so they would not get badly hurt if they crashed. The first flight was 12 seconds long. The fourth flight covered 852 feet in 59 seconds. The Wright brothers had made history. They were the first people to fly a heavier-than-air machine with an engine.

Title and author:

Who flew?

Where?

When?

Why are the Wright brothers famous?

Size — Are all your tall letters the same size?　　Yes　No

95

3 Apply

Ask students to read and follow the directions about taking notes on a book on student page 95. Remind them to use good spacing as they write.

Have students determine whether their writing is legible in the new size. Ask them to look first at their tall letters, next at their short letters, and then at their letters with descenders. Suggest that students choose one group of letters, such as tall letters, and write several examples of letters of that group, stopping frequently to evaluate.

Proper Size is important. Help students respond to the Key feature at the bottom of student pages 94 and 95. Ask:

- Are your letters made with consistent size?
- Is your writing easy to read?

Handwriting Coach

Spacing Remind students that a little more space is needed before a word that begins with a downcurve letter (**a, d, g, o, c,** and **q**). Write on the board a sentence such as **An alligator gave the ducks quite a scare**. Use colored chalk or markers to indicate the space needed.

Tips From an
Occupational Therapist

Have students write their names in cursive in the middle of a piece of paper. Tell them to use a black marker to draw a line bordering their name that follows the shape of the letters. Instruct students to draw more lines, about an inch apart, until they have drawn lines to the edge of the page. Have students use colored pencils to fill in the borders. Using colored pencils will help with endurance, as they require more effort than markers.

T95

Write for Someone Else

Objective: To practice writing a phone message using legible cursive handwriting.

Write for Someone Else

Sometimes you write things for someone else to read. When you write for someone else, you must be sure that your writing is legible.

Juan took this phone message for his sister.

Thursday

Maria,
Sophia Martin called at 10:00. Your job interview at J.P. Insurance Company will be on Monday at 4:00. Good luck!
Juan

What makes Juan's message legible? Check each true statement.

☐ There is space for O between letters.
☐ There is space for $\backslash$ between words.
☐ There is space for $\mathcal{O}$ between sentences.

Add this message to the pad.

P.S. Call 555-1235 if you can't make it. She'll be in the office until 5:00.

On the following pages, you will write a friendly letter, a school paper, an invitation, a thank-you note, and a news story. As you write, you will focus on spacing to help make your writing legible.

96

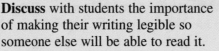

Handwriting Coach

Practice Handwriting practice is most beneficial when it is done in the student's strongest learning modality. Students can take turns saying stroke descriptions so auditory learners can write what they hear. Visual learners benefit from accessible, prepared models. Kinesthetic learners enjoy forming letters with ropes of clay.

1 Present the Activity

Discuss with students the importance of making their writing legible so someone else will be able to read it.

Read aloud the background information on student page 96. Discuss experiences students might have had with illegible messages they wrote for themselves or others have written for them. Encourage volunteers to describe how legibly written messages have been helpful.

2 Write and Evaluate

Have students read and follow the directions for writing and evaluating on student page 96. Help students as needed to complete the activity on the page.

✔ **Use** these questions to help students evaluate their cursive writing:
- Does your writing have uniform forward slant?
- Did you allow correct spacing between letters, words, and sentences?

Support for English Language Learners

Some students may need help with writing a phone message. Point out the parts to the message: **day, name of person, message,** and **signature of person writing note.** Write the terms on the board. Have volunteers come to the board and write an example next to each heading. Some students might also need help with the abbreviation *P.S.* Tell them that it means *postscript,* a message or note added as an afterthought to a note or message.

T96

Write a Friendly Letter

Read this friendly letter. Notice its five parts.

> *581 Ashley Court*
> *Hickory, North Carolina 28601* — heading
> *March 5, 20 ____*
>
> *Dear Brittany,* — greeting
>
> *Great news! I got a puppy! I named her*
> *Button because she is small and round. She* — body
> *has fluffy brown fur and cute little ears.*
> *I heard you made the track team. Good work!*
>
> *Your friend,* — closing
> *Nica* — signature

Write the body of a letter to a friend. Pay attention to the spacing between letters, words, and sentences. You can copy the one above, or you can write your own.

Spacing

Is there proper spacing between letters?	Yes	No
Is there proper spacing between words?	Yes	No
Is there proper spacing between sentences?	Yes	No

97

Objective: To practice writing a friendly letter using legible cursive handwriting.

1 Present the Activity   2 Write and Evaluate

Read with students the instructions and the friendly letter on student page 97. Help them identify the five parts of a friendly letter. Ask them to describe the information each part contains.

Encourage students to describe a time when they received a friendly letter from a friend or relative whose writing was difficult to read. Ask volunteers to describe the importance of legibility in friendly letters.

Ask students to write the body of a letter to a friend, remembering to focus on making their writing legible.

Proper Spacing fosters legibility. Help students respond to the Key feature at the bottom of student page 97. Ask:

- Did you leave the correct amount of spacing between letters?
- Are your letters neither too far apart nor too close together?

Content Connection

Language Arts

Ask students to imagine they have gone on a family vacation. Have them write a friendly letter to a friend or a relative back home, telling them about their vacation experience. Alternatively, they might write to a friend they met while on vacation, telling them what a good time they had on the trip. Remind them to include the five parts of a friendly letter (*heading, greeting, body, closing, and signature*).

T97

Write for School

Objective: To practice writing a heading, title, and paragraph using legible cursive handwriting.

Write for School

When you write for school, you usually write a heading and a title on your paper. The heading might contain your name, your teacher's name, the subject, and the date.

Write the paragraph to complete Taylor's paper.

Our class should visit the aquarium. We can get there by bus. We could see the giant saltwater tank. We might see the sharks being fed

Taylor Sheets
Mrs. Johnson
Science
April 17
    My Idea for a Class Trip

My writing has good ☐
My writing has good ☐
My writing has good ☐
My writing has good ☐

98

Handwriting Coach

Using the Board Continue to use the board for teaching and practicing basic strokes, letters, and numerals. Students who have difficulty with their motor skills might benefit from the increased space the board provides. Since erasing is easy, identification and correction of errors becomes a simpler task.

1 Present the Activity

Read aloud the background information at the top of student page 98. Discuss experiences students have had when part of a heading they wrote was illegible.

Encourage volunteers to describe how a legibly written heading is helpful to both students and teachers.

2 Write and Evaluate

Have students read the directions and complete the writing activity on student page 98.

Proper Shape, Size, Spacing, and Slant make words easy to read. Ask:

- Do your letters look like the models?
- Are your short letters half the height of your tall letters?
- Is there proper space between each letter, word, and sentence?
- Did you use proper slant?

Support for English Language Learners

Some students might need some help identifying and writing ideas for a class trip. Write several categories on the board, such as **Museums, Parks, Aquariums,** and **Special Attractions**. Have students think of and name places they know that fit into these categories. Write their responses on the board. Then ask them to complete the writing activity on student page 98.

T98

Complete the heading on this paper. Then write a paragraph about a trip that your class could take. Give at least three reasons why the class should take this trip.

Name:

Teacher:

Subject:

Date:

Title:

Spacing

Is there space for O between letters?	Yes	No
Is there space for \ between words?	Yes	No
Is there space for O between sentences?	Yes	No

99

3 Apply

Ask students to read and follow the directions for writing a paragraph about a class trip on student page 99.

Have students determine whether their writing is legible. Ask them to describe how good spacing improves the legibility of their writing.

Tell students it is important to make their writing easy for others to read. Remind them to complete all **Stop and Check** activities.

Proper Spacing makes each letter easy to read. Help students respond to the Key feature at the bottom of student pages 98 and 99. Ask:

- Did you write with correct spacing between letters in your words and between your words?
- Did you write with correct spacing between your sentences?

Handwriting Coach

Practice Students who have mastered the skill of writing the lowercase and uppercase cursive letters without models should be given writing activities that will challenge them and require thinking. Reteaching, for any student who still needs it, will be most effective if practice is given in the student's dominant learning modality.

Writing Center

Have students write a narrative about the best possible field trip. First, brainstorm with students about what they think makes a trip successful. Then have students write a personal narrative about their ides for a successful trip. Encourage them to include ideas from the brainstorming session.

T99

Write an Invitation

Objective: To practice writing an invitation using legible cursive handwriting.

Write an Invitation

Use your best handwriting when you write an invitation. Use this information to fill out the party invitation below.

- *The party is for Andrea.*
- *The date is May 25.*
- *The time is 1:00.*
- *The address is 62 Sunset Avenue Wichita Falls, Texas*
- *RSVP by May 15 to 555-7716.*

For:

Date:

Time:

Place:

RSVP:

100

Handwriting Coach

Writing Lines Draw the new writing lines on one side of 9-inch by 12-inch sheets of oak tag and laminate one sheet for each student. Students can use these as "slates" by practicing their smaller handwriting with a wipe-off crayon. The reverse side can be used for such things as letter activities.

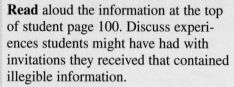

1 Present the Activity

Read aloud the information at the top of student page 100. Discuss experiences students might have had with invitations they received that contained illegible information.

Encourage volunteers to describe the importance of legibly written invitations.

2 Write and Evaluate

Have students read and follow the directions for writing on student page 100. Remind them to write using correct size. Help students as needed to complete the activity on the page.

✓ **Use** these questions to help students evaluate their writing:

- Did you use correct spacing in your writing?
- Do your descenders avoid crashing into the letters below?
- Is your writing legible?

Support for English Language Learners

Some students might need help with filling in the party invitation. Use the questions **Who, What, When, Where** to help students write the party invitation. Explain that *RSVP* is a French expression: *repondez s'il vous plait.* It means "please reply." Ask students when people invited to the party must reply *(by May 15)*.

T100

Write a Thank-You Note

Here is a thank-you note that Andrea wrote after her party.

June 5

Dear Matt,

Thank you for helping me decorate the yard for my party. There was so much to do! The yard looked great. Thank you again.

Your friend,
Andrea

Write Andrea's thank-you note to Matt, or write a note to thank someone who has helped you.

My writing has good
My writing has good
My writing has good
My writing has good

101

Write a Thank-You Note

Objective: To practice writing a thank-you note using legible cursive handwriting.

1 Present the Activity

Read with students the introductory statement and the thank-you note at the top of student page 101.

Encourage them to describe experiences they might have had with thank-you notes they either wrote or received that contained information that was written illegibly. Ask volunteers to describe the importance of legibly written thank-you notes.

2 Write and Evaluate

Ask students to write the thank-you note on the page or their own, remembering to focus on making their writing legible.

Proper Shape, Size, Spacing, and Slant make words easy to read. Ask:

- Do your letters look like the models?
- Are your tall letters twice the height of your short letters?
- Is there proper space between each letter and word?
- Did you use proper slant?

Handwriting Coach

Automaticity The ability to write letters and words automatically allows students to spend more time thinking about the content of their writing. To make sure students are gaining automaticity, ask them to demonstrate correct letter formation with their eyes closed.

Tips From an Occupational Therapist

Encourage parents to help their children practice fine-motor skills at home. Many activities around the house help students improve fine-motor coordination and strength to further improve their handwriting. Students may help with cooking by measuring out ingredients, kneading dough, mixing ingredients, or using cookie cutters. These activities involve fine-motor control and strengthen the finger and hand muscles.

T101

Write a News Story

Objective: To prewrite and brainstorm topics for a news story.

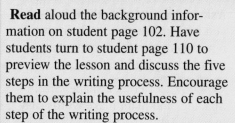

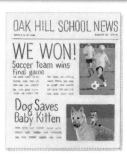

Write a News Story

A news story is a factual report about a current event. It uses facts to tell about the event. A news story does not tell the writer's opinion.

Follow these steps for writing a news story.

I. Prewriting
Start by thinking about a topic for your news story. Imagine that your readers will be the students in your class. **Brainstorm** topics to add to the list below. Write legibly so you can read your ideas later.

school team wins a big game
class visitors
new student in class
school concert
new class pet
school play opens

Look back at your list. Choose your topic. Write the subject of your news story below.

102

Handwriting Coach

Guidelines for Writing Partners

Provide students with a copy of these guidelines when they work with a writing partner.

1. Listen carefully to your partner.
2. Give positive feedback first.
3. Ask questions that will help your partner.
4. Be honest and kind when making suggestions about your partner's work.

1 Present the Activity

Read aloud the background information on student page 102. Have students turn to student page 110 to preview the lesson and discuss the five steps in the writing process. Encourage them to explain the usefulness of each step of the writing process.

Explain that they will use the five steps of the writing process to write a news story for publication. First, they will plan their writing by making a list of possible topics.

2 Write and Evaluate

Have students read and follow the directions for prewriting on student page 102. Help students as needed to add topics to the list on the page.

✓ **Use** these questions to help students evaluate their writing. Ask:
- Can you read your notes?
- Do you have proper spacing between letters and words?
- Does your writing have a uniform slant?

Suggest that they cross out and rewrite any words they might find hard to read later.

Support for
English Language Learners

Some students might need help generating additional topics for a news story. Use the list on the student page to help them brainstorm other newsworthy stories. Examples: **new school desks, new computers, new school building, special visitors speaking to students, an upcoming class field trip**. Encourage students to prepare their list in cursive writing.

Answer the "5W's and H" questions to plan your news story.

What happened?

Who was involved?

When did it happen?

Where did it happen?

Why did it happen?

How did it happen?

News stories start with the most important facts and end with the least important. List facts for your news story from most important to least important.

Most important

Least important

103

1 Present the Activity

Review the meaning of the "5W's and H" questions referred to at the top of student page 103. (**What? Who? When? Where? Why? How?**)

Encourage discussion about the importance of including this information in a news story.

2 Write and Evaluate

Have students read and follow the directions for writing facts on student page 103. Help students as needed to answer the "5W's and H" questions and write the most important and least important facts about their topic.

✓ **Use** these questions to help students evaluate their writing. Ask:

- Did you form your letters carefully so they are easy to read?
- Is there proper space between each letter and word?
- Are your slant strokes pulled toward the baseline?
- Are your letters the correct size?

Handwriting Coach

Brainstorming When pairing students for brainstorming, choose partners whose strengths complement each other's. Actively serve as an adviser to each pair. Assist by giving additional explanations and setting performance time limits. Remind students to follow the brainstorming steps you introduced on page T102.

Content Connection — Technology

Some students might benefit from transferring their notes into an outline. Briefly review the basics and purpose of an outline. Help students prepare an outline from their topic notes using a word processor. Show them how to use the bullets and numbering features of the word processing program. Discuss the usefulness of a word processor in the writing process.

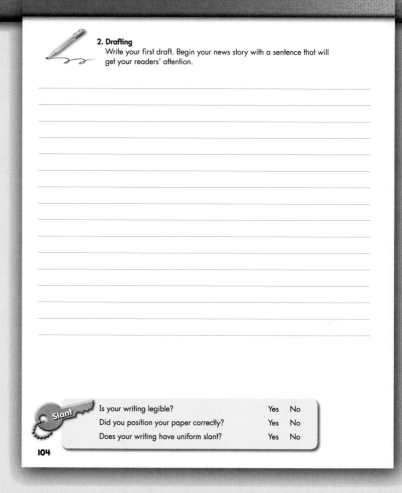

2. Drafting
Write your first draft. Begin your news story with a sentence that will get your readers' attention.

	Is your writing legible?	Yes	No
Slant	Did you position your paper correctly?	Yes	No
	Does your writing have uniform slant?	Yes	No

104

Objective: To write a first draft of a news story using legible cursive handwriting.

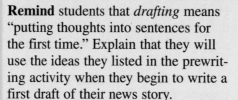

Handwriting Coach

Drafting Students' best handwriting isn't necessary for a first draft. In fact, concentrating too much on handwriting can take students' attention away from the content of their writing. However, a carelessly written draft makes revising and editing more difficult. As students develop a consciousness about legibility, their writing will be more fluent and easy to read.

1 Present the Activity

Remind students that *drafting* means "putting thoughts into sentences for the first time." Explain that they will use the ideas they listed in the prewriting activity when they begin to write a first draft of their news story.

Help students think of a sentence that will grab a reader's attention to begin their news story.

2 Write and Evaluate

Have students read and follow the directions for writing their first draft on student page 104. Help them as needed to begin their first draft. Instruct students to write using complete sentences and leaving space for margins. Remind students to write using correct slant.

✓ **Use** these questions to help student evaluate their writing:

- Can you read your draft?
- Does your writing have consistent forward slant?

Support for
English Language Learners

Because sentence word order is different in different languages, some students might need additional help with the order of words in English sentences. Write the words **subject-verb-object** and the sentence **Vera likes news stories** on the board. Briefly review the meaning of *subject*, *verb*, and *object*. Ask volunteers to name the subject, verb, and object in the sentence. Provide additional examples to reinforce the concept and help students feel confident enough to write their first draft.

T104

3. Revising
Read your draft and mark any changes you want to make. You may want to ask a classmate to help you. Use the editing marks below as you revise your news story.

≡	Make a capital.	∧	Insert or add.
/	Use lowercase.	ℓ	Delete or take out.
⊙	Add a period.	¶	Indent for a new paragraph.

4. Editing
Check your news story for errors in spelling, punctuation, and capitalization. Then answer the questions below to help you check your handwriting. You may want to ask a classmate to help you.

Do your letters have good shape?	Yes	No
Are all your tall letters the same size?	Yes	No
Are your short letters half the size of your tall letters?	Yes	No
Did you avoid collisions?	Yes	No
Is there space for ○ between letters?	Yes	No
Is there space for \ between words?	Yes	No
Is there space for ○ between sentences?	Yes	No
Does your writing have uniform slant?	Yes	No
Is your writing legible?	Yes	No

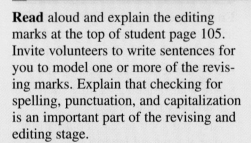
5. Publishing
Use your best handwriting to make a final copy of your news story. Then follow these steps to publish your news story:

- Add a title.
- Add your name as a byline.
- Add an illustration, if you wish.
- Post your story on a bulletin board with everyone else's stories.
- Read the class newspaper!

105

Objective: To revise, edit, and publish a news story using legible cursive handwriting.

Handwriting Coach

Revising, Editing, and Publishing
Along with spelling, punctuation, and other language mechanics, thinking about legibility should always be part of the editing stage of the writing process. You might wish to work as a class to devise editing symbols to use for marking spots on a draft where handwriting needs to be improved.

1 Present the Activity

Read aloud and explain the editing marks at the top of student page 105. Invite volunteers to write sentences for you to model one or more of the revising marks. Explain that checking for spelling, punctuation, and capitalization is an important part of the revising and editing stage.

Continue reading and explaining the last step—publishing—making sure students understand what is required of them as they finalize their news stories. Point out that neat, legible writing shows courtesy to readers, makes a good first impression, and helps ensure that readers will understand the writer's message.

2 Write

Have students follow the steps on student page 105 to revise, edit, and then publish their news stories. Help students determine whether their writing is ready for publication by using the checklist on the page to identify any areas where improvement is needed.

Encourage students to do their personal best as they make a final copy of their work, making sure to incorporate all the changes they marked during revising and editing. Remind them to leave space for margins as they write.

3 Evaluate

Tell students it is important to make their writing easy for others to read.

Use these questions to help students evaluate their writing. Ask:

- Is there proper space between each letter, word, and sentence?
- Did you avoid collisions between tall letters and descenders?
- Is your writing easy to read?

Writing Center

Have students compile the final copies of their news stories into a class newspaper. Remind students that their final copy will need to include a title, a byline, and an illustration. Provide copies for other classes to read.

T105

Writing Quickly

The goal of handwriting instruction is to enable students to write legibly with ease and fluency. It is important, however, not to stress fluency (speed) too early. Students should master writing the lowercase and uppercase alphabets before there is a concern for speed. By the end of fourth grade, students should be able to write legibly, without stress, approximately 50 letters per minute. Based on this estimate, students should be able to write the poem on the page, legibly and without stress, in about one minute and twelve seconds.

Objective: To practice writing quickly and legibly.

Writing Quickly

Writing quickly is a skill that you need to draft a story, write a timed test, or take notes as your teacher talks. Writing that is done quickly should still be easy to read. With practice, you will learn how to make your writing speedy and legible.

Read the lines of poetry below. They are part of a poem written by Julia A. Fletcher Carney in 1845. Write the poem quickly and legibly.

Little drops of water,
Little grains of sand,
Make the mighty ocean
And the pleasant land.

Write the lines of poetry again. Try to write even faster, but make sure your writing is still legible.

106

Handwriting Coach

Why Write Quickly?

Discuss with students times when being able to write quickly might be helpful or necessary. These might include taking notes in class, copying an address or telephone number from TV, jotting down ideas as they come to mind, writing words for a spelling test, and writing a paragraph or a story. Emphasize the importance of maintaining legibility even when writing quickly. Describe a time when you or someone you know wrote important information quickly—and were unable to read it later.

The ability to write letters and words automatically allows students to spend more time thinking about the content of their writing. To make sure students are gaining automaticity, ask them to demonstrate correct letter formation with their eyes closed.

Practice

Direct students to look at the poem on the page and read it with you. Review any letters that still present difficulties for any students. When students seem comfortable with the task, have them write the poem the first time, trying to write more quickly than usual but still writing letters that are easy to read. Then have them write the poem a second time.

Note: To make this a timed writing, have students begin and end at your one-minute signal and then count their letters.

Evaluate

Encourage students to evaluate their letters and words by comparing them to the models. Ask these questions:

- Do your letters have good shape?
- Are your tall letters a little shorter than the writing space?
- Are your short letters about half the size of your tall letters?
- Do your descenders go below the baseline consistently?
- Did you allow correct spacing?
- Does your writing have consistent forward slant?

Support for
English Language Learners

For students whose first language does not use the Roman alphabet, the time needed to achieve handwriting fluency may be longer than that needed by students who have more familiarity with Roman letters and numbers. To build vocabulary and promote ease in writing, label pictures and objects and have students create picture dictionaries.

Write the lines of poetry two more times. Try to write even faster, but keep your writing easy to read.

Now read your final writing. Circle Yes or No to respond to each statement. Then show your writing to another reader, either a classmate or your teacher. Ask that person to circle Yes or No beside each statement.

	My Evaluation		My Classmate's or Teacher's Evaluation	
The writing is easy to read.	Yes	No	Yes	No
The writing has good *Shape*.	Yes	No	Yes	No
The writing has good *Size*.	Yes	No	Yes	No
The writing has good *Spacing*.	Yes	No	Yes	No
The writing has good *Slant*.	Yes	No	Yes	No

107

Writing More Quickly

Direct students to look at the writing space on student page 107. Point out that this space is where they are to write the poem two more times. Encourage students to try to write faster than they did during the other two times, but caution them not to sacrifice legibility for the sake of speed.

Follow the procedure for timed writing recommended earlier in this lesson. Help students evaluate their writing by comparing it to the models and to their previous attempts in this lesson. Then have them respond to the evaluation checklist on the student page.

Practice

Have students write the poem twice in one handwriting lesson and again during the next handwriting lesson. This should prevent students from tiring and enable them to continue to write well and not feel stressed.

Evaluation

Self-evaluation is an important step in the handwriting process. By identifying their own handwriting strengths and weaknesses, students become independent learners. The steps in their self-evaluation process are as follows:

Question Students should ask themselves questions such as these: "Is my slant correct?" "Do my letters rest on the baseline?"

Compare Students should compare their handwriting to the models.

Evaluate Students should determine strengths and weaknesses in their handwriting based on the Keys to Legibility.

Diagnose Students should diagnose the cause of any difficulties. Possible causes include incorrect paper or pencil position, inconsistent pressure on the pencil, and incorrect strokes.

Improve Self-evaluation should include a means of improvement through additional instruction and continued practice.

Writing Center

To reinforce both cursive and manuscript writing, have students do many different kinds of writing. Activities might include the following:

- Label pictures and objects.
- Make lists of things in categories.
- Write about field trips.
- Write facts.
- Retell a story in writing.
- Write about books.
- Write the names of friends and pets.

- Write stories, poems, and descriptions.
- Prepare invitations to parties.
- List games and food for parties.
- Send holiday greetings to parents, family members, and friends.

T107

Writing Easily

Now that students have been introduced to the formation of all the cursive letters, they can begin to increase the ease with which they write. The ability to write letters and words automatically allows students to spend more time thinking about the content of their writing.

Objective: To practice writing easily and legibly.

Writing Easily

As you write stories and essays for school papers and tests, it is important that your handwriting flows easily. When you automatically know how to write legibly, you don't have to worry about your handwriting. You are free to think about what you want your writing to say. With practice, you will learn how to make your writing easy, quick, and legible.

Read the writing prompt below. Respond to it by writing on the lines. Let your handwriting flow easily as you think and write.

Descriptive Writing

Think about something interesting you have seen.

Write a description of what you saw.
Include details to help the reader see
what you are describing.

108

Handwriting Coach

To foster students' ability to write easily, have them take notes or dictation as you read specific information aloud. This might be a set of short sentences containing some of their spelling words or it could be a list of facts or information for a science or social studies lesson. Inform them that you will read each item only once, so they are to listen carefully and write what you say. When the exercise is completed, encourage students to evaluate their handwriting.

1 Present the Activity

Direct students to the background information and the writing prompt on student page 108. Encourage discussion about the specific genre being used (descriptive writing), and have volunteers name and describe the writing process steps to help them begin planning their writing.

2 Practice

Have students respond to the prompt on the page by writing a description of a place they have visited. Point out that the writing space continues on the following page. Remind students to leave room for margins.

Support for
English Language Learners

Encourage students to draw pictures before they begin writing. Model by making your own drawing that shows character, setting, and plot. Point to each element of your picture as you describe it. Explain that the picture shows where the story is taking place, or its setting. The picture also identifies the characters and shows the action. Tell students that as a prewriting activity, they can use a picture to help them organize their ideas.

Now read your final writing. Circle Yes or No to respond to each statement. Then show your writing to another reader, either a classmate or your teacher. Ask that person to circle Yes or No beside each statement.

	My Evaluation		My Classmate's or Teacher's Evaluation	
The writing is easy to read.	Yes	No	Yes	No
The writing has good Shape.	Yes	No	Yes	No
The writing has good Size.	Yes	No	Yes	No
The writing has good Spacing.	Yes	No	Yes	No
The writing has good Slant.	Yes	No	Yes	No

109

3 Evaluate

Point out the evaluation checklist on student page 109. Read the statements with students, and encourage them to evaluate their writing and respond to the evaluation comments. Then have them refer to a classmate or to you for additional evaluation.

Tips From an
Occupational Therapist

Students who have difficulty using the eraser on their pencil efficiently will benefit from this activity. Make ten small circles on a piece of writing paper. Have the student color in the first circle, rotate the pencil by turning it with the thumb and fingertips of the writing hand so the eraser is pointing down, erase the second circle, and so on.

Handwriting and the Writing Process

As students participate in the writing process, let them know that good handwriting is always important. Notes, Webs, story drafts, and published pieces that are easy to read cut down on confusion in the classroom and help students express their ideas clearly and confidently.

Review with students the five steps in the writing process identified on student page 110. Encourage discussion on the usefulness of each step as students develop their writing.

Objective: To practice handwriting and the steps of the writing process.

Handwriting and the Writing Process
Write a Paragraph

A paragraph is a group of sentences about one subject. Use the steps below to write a paragraph about how to play your favorite game.

1. Prewriting
Prewriting means gathering ideas and planning before you write. List your ideas on a piece of paper. Then plan your paragraph, telling the subject and in what order you will write your ideas.

2. Drafting
Drafting means putting your thoughts into written sentences for the first time. Use the ideas you listed in Prewriting to draft your paragraph. Write your first draft.

3. Revising
Revising means changing your writing to make it say exactly what you mean. Read your draft. Mark any changes you want to make.

Does your writing include all the information readers want to know?	Yes No
Does your writing include descriptive details?	Yes No

4. Editing
Editing means checking your revised writing for errors in spelling, punctuation, capitalization, and handwriting.

Are all words spelled correctly?	Yes No
Have you used uppercase letters and punctuation correctly?	Yes No
Do your letters have good shape and size?	Yes No
Is there good spacing between letters, words, and sentences?	Yes No
Does your writing have uniform slant?	Yes No
Is your writing easy to read?	Yes No

5. Publishing
Publishing means using your best handwriting to make an error-free copy of your writing. Share your writing.

110

Prewriting
What should I write?

During prewriting, students plan for their writing by making notes, lists, and Webs. Carelessly written prewriting work can cause confusion throughout the writing process, but easy-to-read notes and Webs smooth the way for students, teachers, and writing partners.

Drafting
I write my ideas in sentences.

Students' best handwriting isn't necessary for a first draft. In fact, concentrating on handwriting might take students' attention away from the content of their writing. However, an overly sloppy draft makes revising and editing more difficult. As students develop a consciousness about legibility, their writing will be fluent and easy to read.

Revising
What should I change?

As students revise their drafts, remind them to begin each sentence with an uppercase letter and to use end marks. The revising stage is also a good time to check slant and spacing in the writing. As they revise, students should continue to be aware of the need for legibility.

Editing
How can I improve my spelling and handwriting?

To complete the writing process, have students edit their drafts, checking spelling, punctuation, and handwriting. Thinking about legibility should always be part of the editing stage of the writing process. The Keys to Legibility—Shape, Size, Spacing, and Slant—help students know what to look for.

Publishing
How will I share my work?

When preparing writing for publishing, it's especially important for students to use their best handwriting. Neat, legible writing shows courtesy to readers. It makes a good first impression, and it helps ensure that readers will understand the writer's message.

Support for
English Language Learners

The writing process can be intimidating for some students. Have students complete prewriting activities, such as brainstorming, in their first language. Then help them create comparable lists of English words and phrases. This strategy prevents a limited English vocabulary from stifling creativity.

T110

Record of Student's Handwriting Skills

Cursive

	Needs Improvement	Shows Mastery		Needs Improvement	Shows Mastery
Sits correctly	❑	❑	Writes the undercurve-to-downcurve joining	❑	❑
Holds pencil correctly	❑	❑	Writes the undercurve-to-overcurve joining	❑	❑
Positions paper correctly	❑	❑	Writes the overcurve-to-undercurve joining	❑	❑
Writes numerals 1–10	❑	❑	Writes the overcurve-to-downcurve joining	❑	❑
Writes undercurve letters: *i, t, u, w, e, l*	❑	❑	Writes the overcurve-to-overcurve joining	❑	❑
Writes undercurve letters: *b, h, f, k, r, s, j, p*	❑	❑	Writes the checkstroke-to-undercurve joining	❑	❑
Writes downcurve letters: *a, d, g, o, c, q*	❑	❑	Writes the checkstroke-to-downcurve joining	❑	❑
Writes overcurve letters: *n, m, y, x, v, z*	❑	❑	Writes the checkstroke-to-overcurve joining	❑	❑
Writes downcurve letters: *A, O, D, C, E*	❑	❑	Writes in the new size	❑	❑
Writes curve forward letters: *N, M, H, K, U, Y*	❑	❑	Writes with correct shape	❑	❑
Writes curve forward letters: *Z, V, W, X*	❑	❑	Writes with correct size	❑	❑
Writes overcurve letters: *I, J, Q*	❑	❑	Writes with correct spacing	❑	❑
Writes doublecurve letters: *T, F*	❑	❑	Writes with uniform slant	❑	❑
Writes undercurve-loop letters: *G, S, L*	❑	❑	Writes legibly for self	❑	❑
			Writes legibly for someone else	❑	❑
Writes undercurve-slant letters: *P, R, B*	❑	❑	Writes legibly for publication	❑	❑
Writes the undercurve-to-undercurve joining	❑	❑	Regularly checks written work for legibility	❑	❑

III

Record of Student's Handwriting Skills

The **Record of Student's Handwriting Skills** serves to indicate each student's progress in mastering the skills presented. The chart lists the essential skills in the program. After the skills that are listed have been practiced and evaluated, you will be able to mark the **Record of Student's Handwriting Skills** as either *Shows Mastery* or *Needs Improvement*.

Objective: To indicate each student's progress in handwriting skills.

Needs Improvement

If a student has not mastered a skill, provide additional basic instruction and practice. First, determine the student's specific needs. Then return to the initial teaching steps of the lesson for ways to help the student. To improve letterforms, have the student practice writing the letter both in isolation and within words and sentences. Reinforce instruction through activities geared to the student's modality strengths. Ask the student to evaluate his or her writing with you. Reevaluate the student's writing following practice over time. When the student achieves mastery of the skill, check *Shows Mastery*.

Note: *The* **Record of Student's Handwriting Skills** *is reproduced on* **Practice Master 55***.*

Shows Mastery

Mastery of written letterforms is achieved when the student writes the letters using correct basic strokes. Compare the student's written letterforms with the letter models shown in the book. Keep in mind the Keys to Legibility (Shape, Size, Spacing, and Slant) when evaluating letters, numerals, punctuation marks, words, and sentences for mastery of skill. Observation will indicate whether a student has mastered such skills as pencil and paper position.

Check the appropriate box for each skill.

TIII

Scope and Sequence

	Grade K	Grade I	Grade 2M	Grade 2C (Manuscript/Cursive)
Basic Strokes	17–38	16–23	12–15, 16–17	12–13/56–59, 60, 66–67, 110–111
A	51, 55, 64, 82, 100, 108	62–63, 66	38–39, 40, 84	20–21/112, 118, 154
a	52, 55, 56, 72, 92, 109	62–63, 66	36–37, 40, 84	20–21/88, 94, 106
B	77, 81, 82, 100, 108	92–93, 96	62–63, 68, 84	30–31/149, 150, 154
b	78, 81, 92, 109	92–93, 96	60–61, 68, 84	30–31/74, 76, 106
C	57, 63, 64, 82, 100, 108	70–71, 76	46–47, 52, 84	22–23/115, 118, 154
c	58, 63, 72, 92, 109	70–71, 76	44–45, 52, 84	22–23/92, 94, 106
D	53, 55, 64, 82, 100, 108	64–65, 66	38–39, 40, 84	20–21/114, 118, 154
d	54, 55, 56, 72, 92, 109	64–65, 66	36–37, 40, 84	20–21/89, 94, 106
E	59, 63, 64, 82, 100, 108	72–73, 76	46–47, 52, 84	22–23/116, 118, 154
e	60, 63, 72, 92, 109	72–73, 76	44–45, 52, 84	22–23/72, 76, 106
F	61, 63, 64, 82, 100, 108	74–75, 76	46–47, 52, 84	24–25/141, 142, 154
f	62, 63, 72, 92, 109	74–75, 76	44–45, 52, 85	24–25/80, 86, 106
G	65, 71, 82, 100, 108	78–79, 84	50–51, 52, 84	24–25/144, 150, 154
g	66, 71, 72, 92, 109	78–79, 84	48–49, 52, 84	24–25/90, 94, 106
H	89, 91, 100, 108	104–105, 106	66–67, 68, 84	34–35/123, 126, 154
h	90, 91, 92, 109	104–105, 106	64–65, 68, 84	34–35/79, 86, 106
I	43, 47, 48, 64, 82, 100, 108	52–53, 58	34–35, 40, 84	16–17/137, 142, 154
i	44, 47, 56, 72, 92, 109	52–53, 58	32–33, 40, 84	16–17/68, 76, 106
J	67, 71, 82, 100, 108	80–81, 84	50–51, 52, 84	26–27/138, 142, 154
j	68, 71, 72, 92, 109	80–81, 84	48–49, 52, 84	26–27/84, 86, 106
K	103, 107, 108	120–121, 124	78–79, 80, 84	40–41/124, 126, 154
k	104, 107, 109	120–121, 124	76–77, 80, 84	40–41/81, 86, 106
L	41, 47, 48, 64, 82, 100, 108	50–51, 58	34–35, 40, 84	16–17/146, 150, 154
l	42, 47, 56, 72, 92, 109	50–51, 58	32–33, 40, 84	16–17/73, 76, 106
M	87, 91, 100, 108	102–103, 106	66–67, 68, 84	34–35/122, 126, 154
m	88, 91, 92, 109	102–103, 106	64–65, 68, 84	34–35/97, 102, 106
N	85, 91, 100, 108	100–101, 106	66–67, 68, 85	32–33/121, 126, 155
n	86, 91, 92, 109	100–101, 106	64–65, 68, 85	32–33/96, 102, 106
O	49, 55, 64, 82, 100, 108	60–61, 66	38–39, 40, 85	18–19/113, 118, 155
o	50, 55, 56, 72, 92, 109	60–61, 66	36–37, 40, 85	18–19/91, 94, 106
P	79, 81, 82, 100, 108	94–95, 96	62–63, 68, 85	30–31/147, 150, 155
p	80, 81, 92, 109	94–95, 96	60–61, 68, 85	30–31/85, 86, 106
Q	69, 71, 82, 100, 108	82–83, 84	50–51, 52, 85	26–27/139, 142, 155
q	70, 71, 72, 92, 109	82–83, 84	48–49, 52, 85	26–27/93, 94, 106
R	83, 91, 100, 108	98–99, 106	62–63, 68, 85	32–33/148, 150, 155
r	84, 91, 92, 109	98–99, 106	60–61, 68, 85	32–33/82, 86, 106
S	75, 81, 82, 100, 108	90–91, 96	58–59, 68, 85	28–29/145, 150, 155
s	76, 81, 92, 109	90–91, 96	56–57, 68, 85	28–29/83, 86, 106
T	45, 47, 48, 64, 82, 100, 108	54–55, 58	34–35, 40, 85	18–19/140, 142, 155
t	46, 47, 56, 72, 92, 109	54–55, 58	32–33, 40, 85	18–19/69, 76, 106
U	73, 81, 82, 100, 108	88–89, 96	58–59, 68, 85	28–29/125, 126, 155
u	74, 81, 92, 109	88–89, 96	56–57, 68, 85	28–29/70, 76, 106
V	93, 99, 100, 108	110–111, 116	74–75, 80, 85	36–37/130, 134, 155
v	94, 99, 109	110–111, 116	72–73, 80, 85	36–37/100, 102, 106
W	97, 99, 100, 108	114–115, 116	74–75, 80, 85	38–39/131, 134, 155
w	98, 99, 109	114–115, 116	72–73, 80, 85	38–39/71, 76, 106
X	101, 107, 108	118–119, 124	78–79, 80, 85	38–39/132, 134, 155
x	102, 107, 109	118–119, 124	76–77, 80, 85	38–39/99, 102, 106
Y	95, 99, 100, 108	112–113, 116	74–75, 80, 85	36–37/128, 134, 155
y	96, 99, 109	112–113, 116	72–73, 80, 85	36–37/98, 102, 106
Z	105, 107, 108	122–123, 124	78–79, 80, 85	40–41/129, 134, 155
z	106, 107, 109	122–123, 124	76–77, 80, 85	40–41/101, 102, 106
Numerals	115–126, 131–133	11, 34–47, 132–133	26–29, 86–89	42–43/50–51, 108

	Grade 3	Grade 4	Grade 5	Grade 6
Basic Strokes	32–36, 42–44, 66, 77, 96–98, 106, 124, 132	14–15, 16, 23, 57	8	8
A	99, 104	58, 62	44, 46	40, 42
a	67, 74	36, 40	26, 30	22, 26
B	138, 140	79, 80	61, 64	55, 58
b	51, 60	30, 34	17, 18	17, 20
C	102, 104	59, 62	45, 46	41, 42
c	71, 74	38, 40	28, 30	24, 26
D	101, 104	59, 62	45, 46	41, 42
d	68, 74	36, 40	26, 30	22, 26
E	103, 104	60, 62	45, 46	41, 42
e	49, 60	27, 28	16, 18	16, 20
F	129, 130	75, 76	57, 58	51, 52
f	53, 60	31, 34	20, 24	17, 20
G	133, 140	78, 80	60, 64	54, 58
g	69, 74	37, 40	27, 30	23, 26
H	109, 118	66, 68	49, 54	45, 48
h	52, 60	30, 34	17, 18	17, 20
I	125, 130	74, 76	56, 58	50, 52
i	45, 60	25, 28	14, 18	14, 20
J	126, 130	74, 76	56, 58	50, 52
j	57, 60	33, 34	22, 24	19, 20
K	110, 118	66, 68	49, 54	45, 48
k	54, 60	31, 34	20, 24	18, 20
L	135, 140	78, 80	60, 64	54, 58
l	50, 60	27, 28	16, 18	16, 20
M	108, 118	65, 68	48, 54	44, 48
m	79, 84	43, 46	32, 38	28, 34
N	107, 118	65, 68	48, 54	44, 48
n	78, 84	43, 46	32, 38	28, 34
O	100, 104	58, 62	44, 46	40, 42
o	70, 74	37, 40	27, 30	23, 26
P	136, 140	79, 80	61, 64	55, 58
p	58, 60	33, 34	22, 24	19, 20
Q	127, 130	74, 76	56, 58	50, 52
q	72, 74	38, 40	28, 30	24, 26
R	137, 140	79, 80	61, 64	55, 58
r	55, 60	32, 34	21, 24	18, 20
S	134, 140	78, 80	60, 64	54, 58
s	56, 60	32, 34	21, 24	18, 20
T	128, 130	75, 76	57, 58	51, 52
t	46, 60	25, 28	14, 18	14, 20
U	111, 118	67, 68	50, 54	46, 48
u	47, 60	26, 28	15, 18	15, 20
V	114, 118	70, 72	51, 54	47, 48
v	82, 84	45, 46	34, 38	30, 34
W	115, 118	71, 72	52, 54	47, 48
w	48, 60	26, 28	15, 18	15, 20
X	116, 118	71, 72	52, 54	47, 48
x	81, 84	44, 46	33, 38	29, 34
Y	112, 118	67, 68	50, 54	46, 48
y	80, 84	44, 46	33, 38	29, 34
Z	113, 118	70, 72	51, 54	46, 48
z	83, 84	45, 46	34, 38	30, 34
Numerals	27, 92–93	52–53	9	9

Scope and Sequence (continued)

	Grade K	Grade I	Grade 2M	Grade 2C
Automaticity		140–141	114–115, 116–117	162–163
Corrective Strategies	T151–T154	T151–T154	T127–T130	T176–T178
Cross-Curriculum Connections	T47, T55, T63, T71, T81, T91, T99, T108, T125	56–57, 67, 77, 85, T9, T13, T25, T27, T29, T31, T47, T59, T97, T107, T117, T125	8–9, 16–17, 18–19, 23, 33, 35, 37, 39, 40, 45, 47, 52–53, 57, 59, 61, 63, 65, 67, 68–69, 73, 75, 77, 80–81, 88–89, 96, 100, 104–105, 110–111, 112–113, T21, T41, T85, T106–T107, T117	17, 19, 21, 23, 25, 27, 29, 31, 33, 35, 37, 39, 41, 42–43, 103, 104–105, 109, 119, 127, 135, 136, 143, 151, 164–165, T25, T45, T49, T69, T75, T81, T87, T89, T97, T101, T109, T113, T121, T125, T129, T141, T147, T153, T157
ELL Support	T13, T15, T17, T19, T21, T23, T25, T27, T29, T31, T33, T35, T37, T41, T43, T45, T47, T49, T51, T53, T55, T57, T59, T61, T63, T65, T67, T69, T71, T73, T75, T77, T79, T81, T83, T85, T87, T89, T91, T93, T95, T97, T99, T101, T103, T105, T107, T110, T115, T117, T119, T121, T123, T125, T127, T131, T133, T135, T137, T139, T141	T9, T11, T13, T15, T17, T19, T21, T23, T25, T27, T29, T31, T35, T37, T39, T41, T43, T45, T47, T51, T53, T55, T57, T59, T61, T63, T65, T67, T69, T71, T73, T75, T77, T79, T81, T83, T85, T87, T89, T91, T93, T95, T97, T99, T101, T103, T105, T107, T109, T111, T113, T115, T117, T119, T121, T123, T125, T127, T129, T133, T135, T137, T139, T141	T9, T11, T13, T15, T17, T19, T21, T23, T29, T33, T35, T37, T39, T41, T43, T45, T47, T49, T51, T53, T55, T57, T59, T61, T63, T65, T67, T69, T71, T73, T75, T77, T79, T81, T83, T85, T87, T89, T91, T95, T97, T99, T101, T103, T105, T107, T109, T111, T113, T115, T117	T8, T12, T13, T14, T16, T18, T20, T22, T24, T26, T28, T30, T32, T34, T36, T38, T40, T42, T44, T48, T50, T52, T55, T56, T57, T58, T59, T60, T61, T62, T63, T66, T68, T70, T72, T74, T76, T78, T80, T82, T84, T86, T88, T90, T92, T94, T96, T98, T100, T102, T104, T106, T108, T110, T112, T114, T116, T118, T120, T122, T124, T126, T128, T130, T132, T134, T136, T138, T140, T142, T144, T146, T148, T150, T152, T154, T156, T160, T164
Evaluation	11, 16, 41–46, 49, 50–54, 57–62, 65–70, 73–80, 83–90, 93–98, 101–106, 110–111, 115–124, 127–128, 143	8–9, 15, 17, 19, 20, 21, 23, 34–37, 44, 45, 50–57, 59, 60–65, 67, 69, 70–75, 77–83, 85, 87–95, 97–105, 107, 109, 110–115, 117–123, 125, 127, 128–129, 131, 133, 135, 143, T137, T141	5, 8–9, 12–15, 26, 27, 32–39, 43–51, 53, 55–67, 69, 71–79, 81, 83, 84–85, 87, 89, 90–91, 97, 99, 101, 103, 105, 107, 109, 111, 113, 115, 117, 119	8–9, 16–45, 56–59, 66–75, 77, 79, 80–85, 87–93, 95–101, 103, 105, 107–117, 119, 121–126, 127–133, 135, 137–141, 143–149, 151, 153, 155–157, 163, 165, 167
Handwriting Coaching Tips	T8, T10, T12, T14, T16, T18, T20, T22, T24, T26, T28, T30, T32, T34, T36, T40, T42, T44, T48, T50, T52, T56, T58, T60, T64, T66, T68, T72, T74, T76, T78, T82, T84, T86, T88, T92, T94, T96, T100, T102, T104, T108, T109, T118, T122, T126, T130, T132, T134, T138, T140	T8, T10, T12, T14, T16, T18, T20, T22, T24, T26, T28, T30, T50, T52, T54, T56, T60, T62, T64, T68, T70, T72, T74, T78, T80, T82, T86, T88, T90, T92, T94, T98, T100, T102, T104, T108, T110, T112, T114, T118, T120, T122, T126, T128, T132, T134, T136, T138, T140	T8, T10, T12, T14, T16, T22, T34, T38, T42, T44, T50, T54, T58, T64, T70, T72, T76, T82, T88, T90, T94, T98, T100, T102, T104, T108, T110, T112, T114, T116	T9, T10, T14, T48, T50, T52, T54, T60, T62, T66, T78, T104, T106, T110, T117, T120, T136, T152, T156, T160, T162, T163, T164, T165
Keys to Legibility		15, 24–25, 26–27, 28–29, 30–31, 41, 53, 55, 57, 61, 65, 68–69, 71, 73, 75, 79, 83, 86–87, 89, 91, 93, 95, 101, 105, 108–109, 111, 113, 115, 117, 119, 121, 123, 125, 126–127, 131, 133, 135, T51, T63, T81, T99, T103, T135, T137	5, 16–17, 18–19, 20–21, 22–23, 33, 35, 37, 39, 42–43, 45, 47, 49, 51, 54–55, 57, 59, 61, 63, 65, 67, 70–71, 73, 75, 77, 79, 82–83, 85, 87, 89, 91, 101, 103, 105, 107, 109, 111, 113, 117, T95, T97, T99	5, 14–15, 17, 19, 21, 23, 25, 27, 29, 31, 33, 35, 37, 39, 41, 45, 60–63, 69, 71, 73, 79, 81, 83, 85, 89, 91, 93, 97, 99, 101, 104–105, 107, 109, 113, 115, 121, 123, 125, 126, 129, 131, 137, 139, 141, 145, 147, 149, 152–153, 155, 157, 165
Manuscript Maintenance				
Margin/Indent Practice			41, 42–43, 53, 54–55, 69, 70–71, 81, 82–83, 89, 90–91, 101, 103, 105, 107, 109, 111, 114–115, 116–117	120, 136, 152, 160–161, 162–163, 164–165
Occupational Therapist Tips	T13, T15, T17, T19, T21, T23, T25, T27, T29, T31, T33, T35, T37, T41, T43, T45, T47, T49, T51, T53, T55, T57, T59, T61, T63, T65, T67, T69, T71, T73, T75, T77, T79, T81, T83, T85, T87, T89, T91, T93, T95, T97, T99, T101, T103, T105, T107, T110, T115, T117, T119, T121, T123, T125, T127, T131, T133, T135, T137, T139, T141	T9, T11, T13, T15, T17, T19, T21, T23, T25, T27, T29, T31, T35, T37, T39, T41, T43, T45, T47, T51, T53, T55, T57, T59, T61, T63, T65, T67, T69, T71, T73, T75, T77, T79, T81, T83, T85, T87, T89, T91, T93, T95, T97, T99, T101, T103, T105, T107, T109, T111, T113, T115, T117, T119, T121, T123, T125, T127, T129, T133, T135, T137, T139, T141	T9, T11, T13, T15, T17, T19, T21, T23, T29, T33, T35, T37, T39, T41, T43, T45, T47, T49, T51, T53, T55, T57, T59, T61, T63, T65, T67, T69, T71, T73, T75, T77, T79, T81, T83, T85, T87, T89, T91, T95, T97, T99, T101, T103, T105, T107, T109, T111, T113, T115, T117	T15, T17, T23, T29, T35, T41, T53, T67, T73, T79, T85, T91, T95, T103, T105, T111, T117, T123, T133, T139, T145, T151, T161
Positions: Paper, Pencil, Sitting	12–15, T10–T11	12–13	10–11, 23	10–11, 54–55, 63
Writing Connections	134–135, 136–137, 138, 139, 140, 141–142, T5, T113, T129, T131–T132	51, 53, 55, 57, 59, 61, 63, 65, 67, 71, 73, 75, 77, 79, 80, 83, 85, 89, 91, 93, 95, 97, 99, 101, 103, 105, 107, 111, 113, 115, 117, 119, 121, 123, 125, 128, 129, 131, 135, 138, 142, T7, T33, T49, T68–T69, T86–T87, T108–T109, T126–T127, T132–T133, T134, T137	17, 19, 21, 23, 26, 27, 29, 33, 35, 37, 39, 41, 45, 47, 49, 51, 53, 57, 59, 61, 63, 65, 67, 69, 73, 75, 77, 79, 81, 86, 94–95, 96–97, 98–99, 100–101, 102–103, 104, 105, 106–107, 108–109, 110–111, 112–113, 116–117, 118, T43, T55, T71, T83	17, 19, 21, 23, 25, 27, 29, 31, 33, 35, 37, 39, 41, 77, 78, 87, 95, 103, 119, 120, 127, 135, 136, 143, 160–161, 164–165, 166, T7, T9, T27, T42–T43, T47, T51, T65, T71, T83, T93, T99, T107, T115, T131, T137, T149, T155, T159, T163

	Grade 3	Grade 4	Grade 5	Grade 6
Automaticity	152–153, 154–155, 156–157	106–107, 108–109	90–91, 92–93	74, 75, T76–T77
Corrective Strategies	T167–T170	T119–T122	T103–T106	T87–T90
Cross-Curriculum Connections	18, 61, 74–75, 84, 85, 94–95, 122–123, 130, 131, 139, 144–145, T11, T17, T25, T27, T45, T49, T51, T55, T57, T63, T67, T71, T75, T77, T81, T83, T87, T95, T97, T99, T101, T105, T107, T109, T113, T117, T119, T125, T129, T135, T137, T141, T143, T147, T153	28, 29, 40, 41, 42, 46, 47, 51, 52–53, 62, 63, 68, 69, 72, 76, 77, 80, 81, 85, 90, 94, 95, T11, T25, T37, T43, T49, T57, T69, T75, T81, T87, T88, T91, T97, T103	18, 23, 24, 30, 38, T11, T19, T25, T31, T37, T47, T53, T59, T65, T77, T83, T89	20, 26, 34, 42, 48, T11, T19, T25, T31, T43, T49, T55, T61, T67, T73
ELL Support	T9, T10, T12, T14, T16, T18, T24, T26, T28, T31, T32, T33, T34, T35, T36, T37, T38, T39, T42, T44, T46, T48, T50, T52, T54, T56, T58, T59, T60, T62, T65, T66, T68, T70, T72, T74, T76, T78, T80, T82, T84, T86, T89, T90, T93, T94, T96, T98, T100, T102, T104, T106, T108, T110, T112, T114, T116, T118, T120, T122, T124, T126, T128, T130, T132, T134, T136, T138, T140, T142, T144, T146, T148, T152, T156, T158	T10, T14, T16, T17, T18, T19, T22, T24, T26, T28, T30, T32, T34, T36, T38, T40, T42, T44, T46, T48, T50, T52, T56, T58, T60, T62, T64, T66, T68, T70, T72, T74, T76, T78, T80, T82, T84, T86, T90, T92, T94, T96, T98, T100, T102, T104, T106, T108, T110	T8, T10, T14, T16, T18, T20, T22, T24, T26, T28, T30, T32, T34, T36, T38, T40, T44, T46, T48, T50, T52, T54, T56, T58, T60, T62, T64, T66, T68, T70, T74, T76, T78, T80, T82, T84, T86, T88, T90, T92	T8, T10, T14, T16, T18, T20, T22, T24, T26, T28, T30, T32, T34, T36, T40, T42, T44, T46, T48, T50, T52, T54, T56, T58, T60, T64, T66, T68, T70, T72, T74, T76
Evaluation	5, 10–17, 19, 22–23, 32–35, 42–59, 61, 65–73, 75, 77–83, 85, 87, 89, 92, 96–103, 105–117, 119, 123–129, 131–138, 141, 145, 148–149, 153, 155, 157, 159	5, 8–9, 11, 14, 15, 19, 22, 25–27, 30, 31–33, 35–39, 41, 43–45, 47, 49, 50, 56, 58, 59, 60, 61, 63, 65–67, 69–71, 74, 75, 78, 79, 83, 86–87, 92, 93, 95–99, 102, 104, 107, 109, 111, T90, T91, T105	6, 7, 14–22, 24, 26–28, 30–34, 38, 39, 41, 44, 46, 48, 50, 52, 54–56, 58–60, 63, 64, 67, 71, 75–83, 86, 87, 89, 91, 93–95	6, 7, 14–20, 22–24, 26, 28, 29, 30, 33, 34, 35, 40–42, 44–52, 54, 55, 58, 59, 65–69, 71–73, 75, 77–79
Handwriting Coaching Tips	T9, T23, T36, T38, T64, T86, T122, T144, T154, T155, T157	T8, T9, T10, T11, T16, T18, T24, T48, T82, T86, T87, T90, T91, T92, T93, T95, T96, T98, T99, T100, T101, T102, T103, T104, T105, T106, T108	T7, T9, T10, T11, T23, T29, T35, T36, T40, T53, T62, T70, T84, T86, T88, T90, T92	T7, T9, T11, T31, T60, T64, T66, T74, T76
Keys to Legibility	5, 9, 36–39, 44, 45, 47, 49, 51, 53, 55, 57, 64–65, 66, 67, 69, 71, 77, 79, 81, 83, 86–87, 89, 98, 99, 101, 103, 106, 107, 109, 111, 113, 115, 122–123, 124, 125, 127, 129, 132, 135, 137, T144–145, T10, T11, T12, T13, T14, T15, T16, T17, T64–T65, T86–T87, T122–T123, T144–T145	5, 16–19, 25, 27, 31, 33, 37, 43, 45, 48–49, 59, 65, 67, 71, 75, 79, 82–83, 92, 93, 95, 97, 99, 104, 107, 109, T90, T91, T96, T98, T102	6, 10–11, 14, 16, 18, 20, 22, 24, 26, 28, 30, 32, 34, 38, 40–41, 44, 46, 48, 50, 52, 54, 56, 58, 60, 64, 70–71, 75, 76, 77, 78, 79, 80, 81, 82, 83, 86, 91, 93	6, 10–11, 14, 16, 18, 19, 21, 22, 24, 26, 28, 30, 34, 36–37, 40, 42, 44, 46, 48, 50, 52, 54, 58, 60–61, 65, 66, 67, 68, 69, 71, 75, 77
Manuscript Maintenance	8–9, 10–19, 63, 94–95, 121, 146–147	10, 51, 90	23, 29, 35, 53, 84, 88	25, 31
Margin/Indent Practice	64–65, 105, 122–123, 131, 141, 142, 145, 146–147, T75, T84–T85, T87, T118–T119, T149, T152–T153	29, 35, 41, 47, 62, 63, 64, 68, 69, 76, 83, 91, T80, T81, T85	19, 25, 31, 39, 41, 47, 55, 59, 67, 68, 69, 71, 74, 75, 86, 90–91, 92–93	21, 27, 35, 37, 43, 49, 53, 59, 61, 64, 66, 67, 68, 71, 74–75, 76–77
Occupational Therapist Tips	T15, T23, T29, T43, T47, T53, T61, T69, T73, T79, T85, T91, T103, T111, T115, T121, T123, T127, T133, T139, T145	T15, T23, T31, T35, T41, T47, T53, T61, T67, T73, T79, T85, T95, T101, T109	T9, T17, T23, T29, T35, T39, T45, T51, T57, T63, T69, T75, T81, T87, T93	T9, T17, T23, T29, T35, T41, T47, T53, T59, T65, T71, T77
Positions: Paper, Pencil, Sitting	8, 30–31, 39, T9	12–13, 19	8	8
Writing Connections	19, 61, 62, 75, 76, 85, 105, 119, 120, 131, 141, 142, 152–153, 154–155, 156–157, 158, T9, T13, T21, T41, T65, T87, T145, T151	42, 64, 91, 92–93, 94–95, 96, 97, 98–99, 100, 101, 102–105, 108–109, 110, T27, T33, T39, T45, T51, T59, T65, T71, T77, T83, T107	74, 75, 76, 77, 78, 79, 80, 82, 83, 84, 85–87, 94, T5, T13, T15, T21, T27, T33, T41, T43, T49, T55, T61, T67, T71, T73, T91	66, 67, 68, 70–72, 78

Detailed Cursive Stroke Descriptions

Touch the midline; **downcurve** to the baseline; **undercurve** to the midline. **Slant** to the baseline; **undercurve** to the midline.

Touch the baseline; **undercurve** to the midline. **Slant** to the descender line; **loop back** to the baseline; **overcurve** to the midline. **Lift**. Touch halfway between the midline and the headline; **dot**.

Touch the baseline; **undercurve** to the headline; **loop back; slant** to the baseline; **undercurve** to the midline. **Checkstroke**.

Touch the baseline; **undercurve** to the headline; **loop back; slant** to the baseline. **Overcurve** to the midline; **curve forward** and then **curve under**. **Slant right** to the baseline; **undercurve** to the midline.

Touch just below the midline; **downcurve** to the baseline; **undercurve** to the midline.

Touch the baseline; **undercurve** to the headline; **loop back; slant** to the baseline; **undercurve** to the midline.

Touch the midline; **downcurve** to the baseline; **undercurve** to the headline. **Slant** to the baseline; **undercurve** to the midline.

Touch the baseline; **overcurve** to the midline; **slant** to the baseline. **Overcurve** to the midline; **slant** to the baseline. **Overcurve** to the midline; **slant** to the baseline; **undercurve** to the midline.

Touch the baseline; **undercurve** to the midline; **loop back; slant** to the baseline; **undercurve** to the midline.

Touch the baseline; **overcurve** to the midline; **slant** to the baseline. **Overcurve** to the midline; **slant** to the baseline; **undercurve** to the midline.

Touch the baseline; **undercurve** to the headline; **loop back; slant** to the descender line; **loop forward** to the baseline. **Undercurve** to the midline.

Touch the midline; **downcurve** to the baseline; **undercurve** to the midline. **Checkstroke**.

Touch the midline; **downcurve** to the baseline; **undercurve** to the midline. **Slant** to the descender line; **loop back** to the baseline; **overcurve** to the midline.

Touch the baseline; **undercurve** to the midline. **Slant** to the descender line; **loop back** to the baseline; **overcurve** to the midline; **curve back** to the baseline. **Undercurve** to the midline.

Touch the baseline; **undercurve** to the headline; **loop back; slant** to the baseline. **Overcurve** to the midline; **slant** to the baseline; **undercurve** to the midline.

Touch the midline; **downcurve** to the baseline; **undercurve** to the midline. **Slant** to the descender line; **loop forward** to the baseline. **Undercurve** to the midline.

Touch the baseline; **undercurve** to the midline. **Slant** to the baseline; **undercurve** to the midline. **Lift**. Touch halfway between the midline and the headline; **dot**.

Touch the baseline; **undercurve** to the midline. **Slant right** a little. **Slant** to the baseline; **undercurve** to the midline.

Touch the baseline; **undercurve** to the midline. **Curve down** to the baseline **and back**. **Undercurve** to the midline.

Touch the baseline; **undercurve** to the headline. **Slant** to the baseline; **undercurve** to the midline. **Lift**. Touch just above the midline; **slide right**.

Touch the baseline; **undercurve** to the midline. **Slant** to the baseline; **undercurve** to the midline. **Slant** to the baseline; **undercurve** to the midline.

Touch the baseline; **overcurve** to the midline; **slant** to the baseline; **undercurve** to the midline. **Checkstroke**.

Touch the baseline; **undercurve** to the midline. **Slant** to the baseline; **undercurve** to the midline. **Slant** to the baseline; **undercurve** to the midline. **Checkstroke**.

Touch the baseline; **overcurve** to the midline; **slant** to the baseline; **undercurve** to the midline. **Lift**. **Slant** from the midline to the baseline.

Touch the baseline; **overcurve** to the midline; **slant** to the baseline; **undercurve** to the midline. **Slant** to the descender line; **loop back** to the baseline; **overcurve** to the midline.

Touch the baseline; **overcurve** to the midline; **slant** to the baseline. **Overcurve** and **curve down** to the descender line; **loop** to the baseline; **overcurve** to the midline.

Touch just below the headline; **downcurve** to the baseline; **undercurve** to the headline. **Slant** to the baseline; **undercurve** to the midline.

Touch the midline; **undercurve** to the headline. **Slant** to the baseline. **Retrace** to the headline; **curve forward** to the midline; **loop; curve forward** to the baseline **and back**. **Retrace** slightly; **curve right**.

Touch the headline; **slant** slightly. **Downcurve** to the baseline; **undercurve** to the midline.

Touch the headline; **downcurve** to the baseline; **loop** up to the downcurve line; **curve down** to the baseline **and up** to the headline; **loop; curve right** to the headline.

Touch the headline; **slant** slightly. **Downcurve** to the midline; **loop; downcurve** to the baseline; **undercurve** to the midline.

Touch the headline; **slant** slightly. **Curve forward and right** to the headline. **Lift**. Touch the middle of the curve; **doublecurve** to the baseline; **curve up** to the midline. **Retrace** slightly; **curve right**. **Lift**. Touch the midline; **slide right**.

Touch the baseline; **undercurve** to the headline; **loop** to the midline; **curve forward** to halfway between the headline and midline. **Doublecurve** to the baseline; **curve up** to the midline. **Retrace** slightly; **curve right**.

Touch the headline; **curve forward; slant** to the baseline. **Lift**. Move to the right and touch the headline; **curve back; slant** to the baseline. **Retrace; loop** to the midline; **curve right** to the midline.

Detailed Cursive Stroke Descriptions (continued)

Touch just below the baseline; **overcurve** to the headline; **curve down** to the baseline **and up** to midline. **Retrace** slightly; **curve right**.

Touch just below the baseline; **overcurve** to the headline; **slant** to the descender line; **loop back** to the baseline; **overcurve** to the midline.

Touch the headline; **curve forward; slant** to the baseline. **Lift**. Touch the headline; **doublecurve** to the midline. **Curve forward and down** to the baseline; **undercurve** to the midline.

Touch the midline; **undercurve** to the headline; **loop; curve down** to the baseline; **loop; curve under** below the baseline.

Touch the headline; **curve forward; slant** to the baseline. **Overcurve** past the midline; **slant** to the baseline. **Overcurve** past the midline; **slant** to the baseline; **undercurve** to the midline.

Touch the headline; **curve forward; slant** to the baseline. **Overcurve** past the midline; **slant** to the baseline; **undercurve** to the midline.

Touch the headline; **downcurve** to the baseline; **undercurve** to the headline; **loop; curve right** to the headline.

Touch the midline; **undercurve** to the headline. **Slant** to the baseline. **Retrace** almost to the headline; **curve forward and back** to the slant line.

Touch the baseline; **curve back; overcurve** to the headline; **curve down** to the baseline; **retrace; curve forward** to the baseline; **curve under** below the baseline.

Touch the midline; **undercurve** to the headline. **Slant** to the baseline. **Retrace** almost to the headline; **curve forward and back** to the slant line. **Curve forward** and down to the baseline; **undercurve** to the midline.

Touch the baseline; **undercurve** to the headline; **loop; curve down and up** to the midline. **Retrace** slightly; **curve right**.

Touch the headline; **slant** slightly. **Curve forward and right** to the headline. **Lift**. Touch the middle of the curve; **doublecurve** to the baseline; **curve up** to the midline. **Retrace** slightly; **curve right**.

Touch the headline; **curve forward; slant** to the baseline; **undercurve** to the headline. **Slant** to the baseline; **undercurve** to the midline.

Touch the headline; **curve forward; slant** to the baseline; **undercurve** to the midline; **overcurve** to the headline.

Touch the headline; **curve forward; slant** to the baseline; **undercurve** to the headline. **Slant** to the baseline; **undercurve** to the midline; **overcurve** to the headline.

Touch the headline; **curve forward; slant** to the baseline; **undercurve** slightly past the baseline. **Lift**. Move to the right and touch the headline; **slant** to the baseline.

Touch the headline; **curve forward; slant** to the baseline; **undercurve** to the headline. **Slant** to the descender line; **loop back** to the baseline; **overcurve** to the midline.

Touch the headline; **curve forward and down; slant** to the baseline. **Overcurve** slightly to the baseline; **curve down** to the descender line; **loop** to the baseline; **overcurve** to the midline.

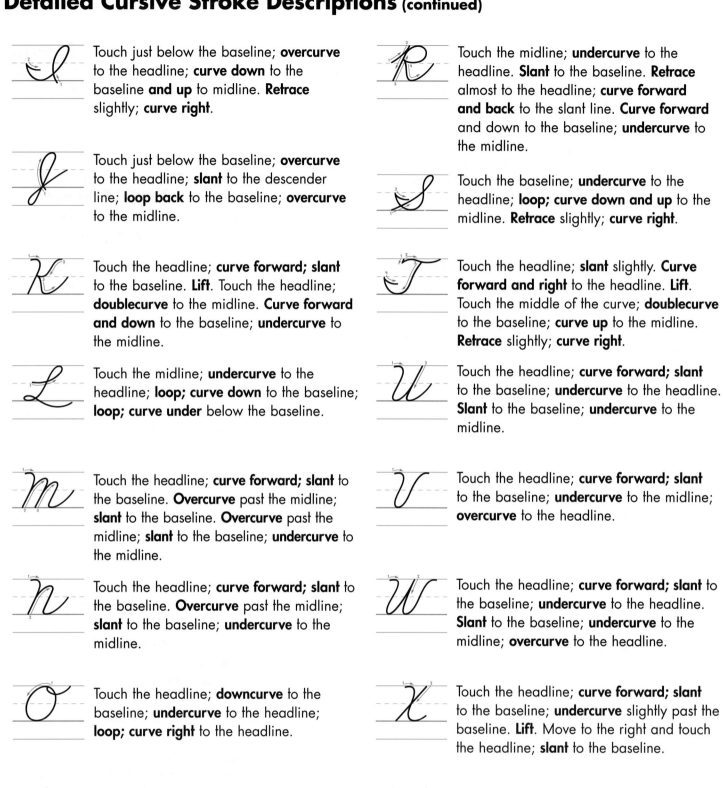

T118

Corrective Strategies for Cursive Letters

a not *a*

Pull the slant stroke toward the baseline with a good retrace.

a not *a*

Pause before writing the slant stroke.

be not *be*

b not *b*

In the checkstroke-to-undercurve joining, deepen the checkstroke before swinging into the undercurve. The second undercurve in **b** ends at the midline.

B not *B*

Make sure the ending stroke touches the slant stroke.

ci not *ci*

Swing wide on the undercurve-to-undercurve joining.

C not *C*

The first stroke is a short slant that begins at the headline.

d not *d*

Pull the slant stroke toward the baseline with a good retrace.

D not *D*

The first loop is open and rests on the baseline.

e not *e*

The loop should be open, not closed.

E not *E*

The bottom downcurve is larger than the top downcurve, and a little farther to the left.

f not *f*

f not *f*

Make sure **f** begins and ends with an undercurve. Close the lower loop near the baseline.

F not *F*

Pause before the retrace.

ga not *ga*

In the overcurve-to-downcurve joining, the overcurve ends at the beginning of the downcurve.

G not *G*

Pause before the retrace.

T119

Corrective Strategies for Cursive Letters (continued)

h not *h*

Close the loop near the midline and keep slant strokes parallel.

H not *H*

Retrace before the loop.

i not *i*

Pull the slant stroke toward the baseline and pause before making the undercurve ending.

l not *l*

Pause after the curve at the midline and retrace slightly.

ji not *ji*

Make sure the overcurve ending stops at the baseline to blend with the undercurve beginning.

j not *j*

Make sure the descender fills the space.

k not *k*

The curve under stroke is followed by a pause, slant right, and undercurve.

K not *K*

Curve forward and down before the undercurve ending.

l not *l*

Close the loop just below the midline.

L not *L*

The lower loop is horizontal and rests on the baseline.

m not *m*

Make sure there is enough space between the overcurves.

M not *M*

Pause after the first and second slant strokes.

N not *N*

Make sure there is enough space between the overcurves.

n not *n*

Make sure the overcurve is round.

oa not *oa*

The checkstroke swings wide to join a downcurve.

O not *O*

Dip the loop down slightly, then curve right to end at the headline.

T120

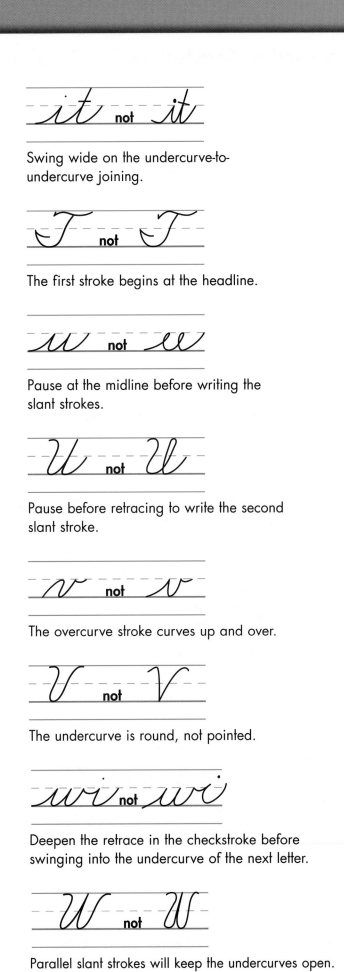

Close the loop near the baseline.

The forward oval curves around and goes below the midline.

Close the loop near the baseline.

The curve under stroke ends below the baseline.

Pause after the first undercurve and then slant right.

Pause at the slant stroke before beginning the second curve forward.

The final undercurve rests on the baseline.

Close the loop at the midline.

Swing wide on the undercurve-to-undercurve joining.

The first stroke begins at the headline.

Pause at the midline before writing the slant strokes.

Pause before retracing to write the second slant stroke.

The overcurve stroke curves up and over.

The undercurve is round, not pointed.

Deepen the retrace in the checkstroke before swinging into the undercurve of the next letter.

Parallel slant strokes will keep the undercurves open.

Corrective Strategies for Cursive Letters (continued)

After writing the overcurve, be sure to slant left toward the baseline.

Pause after the undercurve, to avoid looping.

The second slant stroke crosses the first near the midline.

Close the loop near the baseline.

The overcurve ending crosses the slant stroke at the baseline.

The loop in Z should fill the descender space.

Corrective Strategies for Cursive Writing

Demonstrate the checkstroke joinings and explain the strokes as you write them.

Use the stroke description "retrace and curve right" as students practice these letters.

Point out the letters that change slightly when they are preceded by a checkstroke.

Remind students to begin the downcurve stroke just below the midline. Encourage students to practice deep undercurve strokes to connect with the downcurve strokes.

Instruct students to use ruled paper with a midline or to rule a midline on notebook paper. Explain that short letters should touch the midline.

Show students how to evaluate their writing for size by drawing a horizontal line across the tops of letters that should be the same height.

Remind students to shift both the paper and the hand as the writing progresses. The paper moves toward the student, and the hand moves away. Show students how improving joinings will automatically improve letter spacing.

Remind students to check their paper position and to pull strokes in the proper direction. Show students how to evaluate slant by drawing lines through the slant strokes of their letters. The lines should be parallel.

Checklist for Handwriting Instruction

Developed by Steve Graham, Vanderbilt University

Directions: This checklist is a tool for assessing handwriting instruction. Place a check next to each item that describes a feature of instruction in your classroom. When completed, a review of this checklist can assist you in maintaining and improving the effectiveness of your current handwriting program. It can also help you identify instructional procedures that are effective in improving the legibility and fluency of students who experience difficulty mastering the handwriting process.

I promote handwriting development by

- [ ] making sure that each student—left-handed and right-handed—employs proper sitting, paper, and pencil positions for writing.

- [ ] teaching students to identify and name the letters of the alphabet.

- [ ] allotting approximately 15 minutes per day to handwriting instruction.

- [ ] providing students with plenty of opportunities to use different types of writing instruments and paper.

- [ ] asking students to set goals for improving specific aspects of their handwriting.

- [ ] monitoring students' handwriting, paying special attention to their instructional needs in letter formation, spacing, slant, alignment, size, and line quality.

- [ ] helping students develop a positive attitude about handwriting.

I teach students how to write each letter by

- [ ] showing them how it is formed.

- [ ] describing how it is similar to and different from other letters.

- [ ] using visual cues, such as numbered arrows, as a guide for letter formation.

- [ ] providing practice tracing, copying, and writing the letter from memory.

- [ ] asking them to identify or circle their best formed letter or letters.

- [ ] encouraging them to correct or rewrite poorly formed letters.

- [ ] reinforcing their successful efforts and providing corrective feedback as needed.

I help students become more fluent in handwriting by

- [ ] providing them with plenty of opportunities to write.

- [ ] having them copy a short passage several times, trying to write it a little faster each time.

- [ ] encouraging them to make all final drafts of papers neat and legible.

I assist students who are experiencing difficulty by

- [ ] organizing my class so that I can provide additional handwriting instruction to students who need it.

- [ ] identifying and addressing roadblocks that may impede a student's success in handwriting.

- [ ] talking with parents and soliciting their advice about how to improve their child's handwriting.

- [ ] coordinating my handwriting instruction with the efforts of other professionals, such as an occupational therapist.

- [ ] placing special emphasis on the teaching of difficult letters, such as **a, j, k, n, q, u,** and **z,** as well as reversals.

- [ ] ensuring that the student masters one style of handwriting before introducing a second style.

I make sure that I

- [ ] maintain my belief that I can teach each student in my class how to write fluently and legibly.

- [ ] set high but realistic expectations for the handwriting performance of each student in my class.

- [ ] maintain a balanced perspective on the role of handwriting in learning to write.

Glossary of Handwriting Terms

backward oval
an oval motion made in a counterclockwise direction, as in *a*

baseline
the guideline on which letters rest

basic manuscript strokes
lines that make up all manuscript letters: vertical, horizontal, circle, slant

basic cursive strokes
lines that make up all cursive letters: undercurve, downcurve, overcurve, slant

checkstroke
the modified undercurve that ends *b, o, v* and *w*

circle back line
counter-clockwise circle that begins at 1:00 position

circle forward line
clockwise circle that begins at 9:00 position

continuous-stroke manuscript alphabet
Zaner-Bloser alphabet that requires few or no lifts of the writing tool

cursive
slanted writing in which the letters are connected

descender
the part of a letter that extends below the baseline, as in **g** and *g*

directionality
top-to-bottom and left-to-right movement of eyes, hands, and writing tool when reading and writing

downcurve
a downward counterclockwise motion, such as the beginning stroke in *a*

downstroke
any stroke that is pulled downward

fine motor skills
movements such as grasping, releasing, tearing, cutting, drawing, and writing that depend on development of the small muscles such as those found in the hands and wrists; strength and control of the hand support a student's ability to write

forward oval
an oval motion made in a clockwise direction, as in *p*

grip
method of holding a writing tool; three-finger (tripod) grip is preferred

guideline
a line used for the placement of handwritten letters: headline, midline, baseline

hand preference
tendency to choose one dominant and more skilled hand (right or left) for tasks such as writing or throwing a ball

headline
guideline at the top of the writing space

helper hand
non-dominant or non-writing hand that steadies paper and other materials while dominant hand performs the task

Keys to Legibility
elements used to evaluate handwriting: shape, size, spacing, slant

lowercase letter
letter that is not uppercase or capital, sometimes referred to as a "small" letter

manuscript
writing in which the letters are vertical, are made up of lines and circles, and are not joined

midline
guideline which is halfway between the headline and the baseline

multisensory practice
writing practice that engages auditory, visual, and kinesthetic activities

overcurve
stroke made with an upward clockwise motion, as in n

pull down stroke
a vertical line written from top to bottom

retrace
backtracking or tracing over the same line

reversal
a writer's tendency to confuse letters of mirror-opposite shapes, such as **b** and **d**

shape
the form of a letter, determined by the basic strokes; one of the Keys to Legibility

short letter
letter that doesn't extend above the midline

size
the height of a letter, either short or tall, measured by the space it occupies above the baseline; one of the Keys to Legibility

skywriting
method of using large arm muscles to trace a letter's shape in the air before writing it on paper

slant
degree of tilt, or verticality, in written letters; one of the Keys to Legibility

slide line
horizontal line written from left to right

spacing
the distance between letters, words, and sentences; the distance between lines of writing; one of the Keys to Legibility

tall letter
letter that is of the greatest height from the baseline up; letter that touches the headline (in Grades K–4)

undercurve
a stroke made with an upward counterclockwise motion, as in i

uppercase letter
letter that is not lowercase, sometimes referred to as a capital letter or "big" letter

verticality
degree to which letters are written vertically

Glossary of Handwriting-Related Occupational Therapy Terms

bilateral skill
any activity or skill that requires both sides of the body or both hands to complete successfully

bimanual skill
any activity or skill that requires the use of both hands working cooperatively (e.g., opening a bottle top)

compensation technique
a different (and usually less complex) way to complete an activity

directionality
refers to the way that letters are formed when written on the page (e.g., English writing is read from left to right)

dominant hand
the preferred hand used during writing activities

dynamic movement
this movement refers to the ability of the fingers and wrist to move in a coordinated, yet independent manner; for example, a dynamic pencil grip refers to the ability to use the wrist and fingers to move the pencil, in contrast to moving the pencil using the whole arm while holding the wrist and fingers statically

fine motor endurance
the ability to maintain coordination of small muscle groups (such as in the hands, fingers, and wrists) to complete an activity that may take a long time; in handwriting, it is the ability to maintain a proper grasp pattern and proper writing mechanics over a long period of time or during lengthy writing assignments

fine motor skill
the coordination of small muscle groups (e.g., in the fingers) required to manipulate small objects

gross motor skill
the coordination of large muscle groups required to perform movement (e.g., raising your arms or walking)

hand-eye coordination
the ability to use visual input or information to help guide movements of the hand or arm (e.g., catching a ball)

in-hand manipulation
the ability to hold or move an object within one hand

intrinsic muscles
the deep, small muscles within the hand

letter formation
the ability to correctly connect lines or curves using upward, downward, horizontal, or diagonal movements of the pencil to cohesively create a letter

midline
refers to an imaginary line that runs vertically down the middle of the body; "crossing midline" refers to the action of reaching one's arm across the body to help complete a task presented on the other side of the body (e.g., reaching one's right arm across the body to the left side)

opposition
the movement of the thumb to reach across to connect with the pad of each finger (e.g., when the thumb is opposed to the pointer finger, one can make the "okay" sign)

perceptual skill
the ability to interpret and organize information that is received

prehension
the act of gripping or holding something in one's hand

pressure
the amount of force exerted with the pencil when writing on paper

recessive hand
the non-dominant hand, or the hand not usually used during writing activities

T126

seating adaptation
any substitute made to a current seating position that helps to improve posture, attention, and ultimately handwriting (e.g., sitting on a therapy ball chair or placing an air-inflated disc on a regular school chair)

sensory feedback
any additional information received from the sensory system to further support acquiring a new skill (e.g., tracing letters on a student's back provides the child with tactile sensory feedback to help learn formation of new letters)

spatial skill
the ability to visualize what something looks like (e.g., knowing that a triangle is still a triangle even when it is turned upside down; knowing where to write a letter within the lines on a piece of paper)

stability
(in handwriting) having the firm support and proper alignment of the arm and shoulder needed to produce efficient written output

stereognosis
the ability to recognize items using only the sense of touch

tactile cue
any aid that can be felt that triggers or reminds the student of specific rules or positions to use while writing or performing fine motor tasks

tripod grasp
a holding pattern in which the writing utensil is held between the tips of the thumb and pointer finger with the utensil resting on the middle finger; the thumb and pointer finger should form a circle

visual cue
any aid that can be seen that triggers or reminds the student of specific rules or positions to use while writing or performing fine motor tasks

visual memory
the ability to remember a form/letter/shape after it has been removed from sight; in handwriting, the ability to remember how to correctly form letters without a visual guide

visual-motor integration
the ability to interpret visual information into written output (i.e., the ability to copy from the board in a classroom)

visual perceptual skill
the cognitive ability to correctly interpret visual information

visual tracking
the ability to follow an object through space with the eyes (e.g., tracking a thrown football)

web space
refers to the circular opening that is formed when the tip of the thumb and index finger are touching

weight bearing
any activity that requires one's body to work against gravity while putting pressure on the palms of the hands, arms, and shoulders

When Should I Call the Occupational Therapist?

Developed by Asha Asher, MA OTR/L, FAOTA, M.Ed. (Special Education), Cincinnati, Ohio

Use the following checklist to help you determine when the occupational therapist should be consulted for assistance in remediating specific problems that interfere with a student's handwriting development.

An occupational therapist can help identify and treat underlying problems, facilitate development of handwriting skills, and help devise accommodations to enable the student to successfully participate in classroom activities and the educational process.

If you've tried this...	And this happens... Then consult the OT
Provided chair/desk of the appropriate height (i.e., the student can sit with feet flat on the floor, back snug against the chair back, and the desk slightly higher than the student's elbow)	The student assumes improper posture (e.g., head on the desk, sits on feet, sits at the edge of the chair)
Provided direct instruction of letter formations followed by regular guided practice	Written output is below grade-level expectations in either quality, quantity, or both (e.g., writing is difficult to read, student produces one sentence when peers have produced five sentences)
Allowed the student to experiment with writing tools of differing widths to choose one that the student finds most comfortable to use	Student continues to have an awkward pencil grasp AND written output is below grade-level expectations
Allowed student to experiment with writing paper that has lines of differing widths so the student can choose one that works best for him/her	Quality of student writing does not match grade-level expectations
Provided student with opportunities to refine fine motor control by incorporating various activities in the daily program (i.e., cutting, coloring, using small manipulatives such as peg boards, blocks, construction sets)	Student's fine-motor control is below that of peers (e.g., does not show stable hand preference, quality of student writing does not match grade-level expectations)
Provided opportunities to refine pencil control (vertical, horizontal, circle, oblique cross)	Quality of student writing does not match grade-level expectations (student uses too much or too little pressure, letters are formed from the baseline up, or piecemeal)
Provided adequate handwriting instruction	Quality of student writing does not match grade-level expectations (e.g., reversals beyond grade 2, uneven sizing or spacing of letters, omits or repeats letters)
Provided structured classroom expectations	Student's behavior often deteriorates only when written work is required

TI28

Index

Index (continued)